The Forgotten Mourners, Second Edition

The Forgotten Mourners, Second Edition

Guidelines for Working with Bereaved Children

Susan C. Smith

Jessica Kingsley Publishers
London and Philadelphia

The right of Susan C. Smith to be identified as author of this work has been asserted by her in accordance with the Copyright, Designs and Patents Act 1988.

First edition by Margaret Pennells and Susan Smith published in 1995 by Jessica Kingsley Publishers.

This edition published in the United Kingdom in 1999 by
Jessica Kingsley Publishers Ltd,
116 Pentonville Road, London
N1 9JB, England

and

325 Chestnut Street,
Philadelphia PA 19106, USA.

www.jkp.com

© Copyright 1999 Susan C. Smith

Library of Congress Cataloging in Publication Data

A CIP catalog record for this book is available from the Library of Congress

British Library Cataloguing in Publication Data

A CIP catalogue record for this book is available from the British Library

ISBN 1 85302 758 8 pb

Printed and Bound in Great Britain by
Athenaeum Press, Gateshead, Tyne and Wear

Contents

Acknowledgement

Thinking about, and actually writing this book has been a difficult task for me because I had to face the prospect of doing it alone; a very important person is missing from this edition. Sadly, Sister Margaret Pennells died in April 1997 from cancer. We had discussed the prospect of a new edition during her illness, but we both knew the task would be too much for her to bear during treatment. Writing this book has, therefore, been part of my grief work which I have not gone through very easily at times. I know this book will be the poorer for not having Margaret's contribution but I hope she would be as proud of it now as we were when it was first written.

Margaret was a very special person and a very special friend to me. She helped me grow professionally and supported me personally through some very difficult times. When we began working together, I was still a naive social-work student with great aspirations. Margaret helped me to shape some of those aspirations; she assisted in honing newly acquired skills, and taught me new ones. She was patient and generous with her time, and for all of this I will always be very thankful.

People who knew Margaret would have agreed she had very special qualities. They endeared her to everyone. She was a woman of exceptional integrity who accepted everyone she met for who they were and respected their individuality. She was a kind, warm, open-hearted person who shared her talents and zest for life with everyone she came into contact with. Margaret's death has left a lot of sad people in its wake, but all of us the more joyful for having known her and shared in her life. Not least of whom are the children she helped in our bereavement groups.

I would like to dedicate this book to the memory of Sister Margaret Pennells, of the Holy Order of The Good Shepherd Sisters. You are with me always.

Sue Smith 1999

Introduction

Since the first edition of *Forgotten Mourners* was published in 1995, our understanding about bereaved children has grown considerably. It is not now a question of whether children grieve, as this is now largely accepted. Now it is a question of how can we recognise grief and how can we help. We have also begun to understand the effects of traumatic grief and how we can alleviate the suffering this causes, and that bereaved children face special issues that bereaved adults either do not face or do not fully comprehend.

The world has learned a lot about bereavement and its effects on both children and adults. This has been brought about by many instances of 'community' grief – reports on our television screens of workers and residents dying in offices and apartment blocks from terrorists bombs, children in schools being shot down by a gunman, or more shockingly by one of their school friends, and of course Britain's own poignant experience of grief following the tragic death of Diana, Princess of Wales. Even if we didn't know the people involved, we are more able to empathise with and understand the intense and overwhelming feelings that bereavement can uncover in any one of us.

Even so, it is still sometimes difficult for adults to imagine that children can experience the range and intensity of emotions that adults feel at times of loss. This may be because children present their feelings differently, often turning them inwards on themselves to spare their grieving families any more hurt. Children can show signs of depression, withdrawal, and nervous anxiety. Others may push their feelings outwards in angry, aggressive and awkward behaviour as they struggle to make sense of their situation and try to handle their feelings. There may be a combination of these presenting behaviours as bereaved children live on an emotional 'see-saw' – up one moment and down the next. At times they may change their attitude to what has happened, swinging from displays of sadness to callous comments. Sometimes the behaviour presented by grieving children is not linked to their bereavement at all and the child ends up labelled as *bad*, when in fact, they are just *sad*.

Little wonder, then, that the adults who try to care for, or work with, bereaved children are confused by their behaviour, and why adults still try to protect children from the pain of grief. We want to spare children the difficult task of having to deal with the emotions and other issues that bereavement can raise. However this denies children the means to overcome their loss and the ability to manage painful situations. In the intervening years since this book was first published a wealth of literature has grown up about the effects of bereavement and trauma on children (only some of which are mentioned here), with some studies showing that some mental health problems have their roots in unresolved or badly handled childhood loss (Black 1978; Weller *et al.* 1988; Kranzler *et al.* 1990; Furman 1986). The work of John Bowlby, although in and out of favour at different times, has clearly shown us the significance of the making and breaking of early emotional bonds and the effects that attachment and loss have on our psychological well-being (Bowlby 1969, 1973, 1979, 1980).

The process of grief, of acknowledging that a death has occurred and expressing the feelings related to that loss, gives us the opportunity to resolve and integrate these issues in our life. If grief and trauma experienced in childhood is handled with sensitivity, responding as soon as possible to a child's individual needs, we have a far better opportunity to enable them to recover from grief and to integrate death as part of their knowledge base for life. Death, of course, is a normal part of our lives, and yet we still try to shy away from it, to avoid talking about it, and often we try to refrain from dealing with it. Yet, if we fail to recognise these events and capitalise on them to help us understand our children better, we may consign them to an unhappy and unfulfilled childhood with the spectre of an even unhappier adulthood ahead.

I intended this edition of *Forgotten Mourners* to be more comprehensive than the first one, including additional information to help with understanding bereaved children's needs and to meeting them. I have covered some new ground, neglected in the first edition, on the secondary losses involved in bereavement and the effects of traumatic bereavement, the latter being a field that much is still being learned about.

This book is intended to encourage caring people to take up the task of helping bereaved children. We all have gifts, skills and talents that can be used and we all have a part to play. A listening ear can be as effective as the most profound piece of therapy. I hope this book will help attune your ears (and eyes) more sharply to the needs of bereaved children.

CHAPTER 1

How Children Grieve

When a bereavement occurs, a child will experience the same range of emotions that adults do, from feelings of shock and disbelief to numbness, despair, anger and guilt. The intensity of these feelings is no less acute either, but children can find it incredibly difficult to identify their emotions and, therefore, have problems in expressing feelings appropriately. Many children I have worked with talk of what amounts to an amorphous blob of feelings somewhere inside of them which they can neither describe nor control, causing them confusion and distress. Often these emotions conflict with one another and the child can find itself crying tears of frustration and anger but often only describes feeling sad. A change in the child's behaviour is often one of the first signs of reaction to bereavement and shows that they are struggling with these feelings.

Reactions

A change in behaviour is a reaction to traumatic events and along with other reactions may be recognised as falling into one of the following categories.

Behaviour

Grieving children seem to have a seething mass of unpredictable emotion which threatens to erupt at any time. Because children often do not have enough intellectual skill to identify and verbalise all of this emotion it tends to erupt in negative behaviour. This serves to reinforce the *bad* label rather than enabling us to recognise the child is acting out *sad* feelings. Some of the most common are:

- Physical and verbal aggression and temper tantrums, sometimes misdirected towards the adults caring for them.

- Mood swings, although very common in adolescents are also common in younger children who are suffering the strain of the emotional see-saw.

- Appetite can suffer when normal family patterns of behaviour are disrupted by grief. Children may also look to food as a source of comfort. *Only drastic changes* to the child's eating pattern should be interpreted as a symptom of distress.

- Sleeping disturbances are quite common; an inability to get off to sleep, disturbed sleep patterns, night waking, bad dreams and being afraid to sleep alone or with the light off.

- Children may become withdrawn as family life, their emotions, even school become too complex and difficult to deal with. They may begin to cling, becoming afraid to leave adults for fear of another awful event taking place.

- Regression to earlier forms of behaviour are often common. Children unconsciously want to go back to a time when life seemed safe and predictable, so they may be found sucking their thumb, using baby talk or generally behaving in a childish manner. Bedwetting is also a regressive behaviour occurring at any time during the process of grief and generally improving when the child has had an opportunity to express their fears and worries.

Health

When we are at a low ebb or under stress our bodies often begin to suffer. Our unconscious mind can bring our emotional pain to the surface in the form of illness. Children are no exception.

- Grieving children become vulnerable to illness, picking up every cough and cold around. Worsening or developing new symptoms of asthma frequently occur.

- Children often complain of non-specific 'aches and pains'. Headaches and tummy aches are a common feature.

- A heightened fear of one's own mortality can lead to hypochondria as children worry about whether they too are about to die.

- In extreme cases children have been known to develop symptoms similar to those experienced by the deceased.

School difficulties

Sometimes school represents a safe haven for bereaved children, somewhere they can escape from real life. They may have a trusted teacher or ancillary worker who can give them the time and attention that may temporarily be lacking at home. However, school can also become a place to fear and some children dread going.

- Children may resort to school refusal because they worry about leaving their grieving parent/s. Sometimes they fear something else may happen in their absence.

- Lack of concentration may make them unpopular with teachers. It may cause them to fall behind in their studies, resulting in the additional burden of extra work.

- Some children completely immerse themselves in school in order to forget their grief. This may result in an increase in achievement and the prospect of becoming a high-performing student. Any sudden and sharp increases in attainment following a bereavement could be a sign of grief but may go unnoticed because of its positive connotations.

- Children very often experience cruelty from other pupils who tease them. This may ultimately lead them to retaliate which reinforces negative labels.

Other reactions

These can include tiredness, lethargy, lack of interest in activities or friends. Their co-ordination skills may deteriorate causing frequent slips and falls because their mind is elsewhere. In an attempt to evade grief children can become restless and feverish in their activity, jumping from one pursuit to another trying to find something to interest them. Equally they may become totally disinterested in all their former pastimes as things have less meaning for them.

By far the most common initial reaction is denial; this cannot be happening, it is all a bad dream. Like adults, children also need the natural anaesthetic of numbness and denial in order to allow their minds the time to take in what has happened. They may deny the person has died by not openly showing signs of grief, continuing with life as before. Children, particularly the very young, have an inability to sustain periods of sadness for any length of time and need to return to their 'normal life' (playing, watching TV, and running about) as a way of coping with the situation. However their denial may be connected to their fears about change and an uncertain future without the deceased, 'If I can pretend this hasn't happened life will be the same as before'. The denial could also be a product of the way in which the rest of the family are dealing with the loss. If the parent/s cannot cope with the loss this can be transferred on to the child who is unconsciously led into maintaining the situation.

Children may also try to protect the adults around them from further pain by not appearing to be affected by the loss. They may suppress their need to cry and act out their distress. Sometimes the child is afraid that showing their grief will make mum or dad feel worse, make them more unhappy or even angry. Sadly sometimes this is true, which reinforces the child's need to deny their feelings. Denying grief can sometimes be born out of fearing the sheer intensity of the emotions experienced. Children fear being overwhelmed by their feelings, that they will never recover, that grief will eat them up, so they try to lock away the pain and ignore it.

Feelings

A child's feelings and reactions to a bereavement are mostly influenced by their perception of themselves and by their perception of what has happened to the deceased. Explanations concerning the death are very important (see Chapter 4) and may affect what a child feels. Some of the most commonly expressed feelings are the following:

Guilt

One way to control the pain of grief is to turn it inwards and blame oneself and children are almost more likely than adults to do this. Children are very egocentric, seeing themselves as all powerful, the centre of the universe and capable of doing many things. Normally this is healthy and helps with a child's curiosity, exploration and self-confidence. However, when a bereavement occurs this egocentric power may become unhealthy and can lead to guilt. A child may blame themselves for not having prevented the death; for not intervening in some way. One boy felt guilty for not persuading his father to go to the doctor's. The child had hoped to prevent the heart attack which later killed his father. Children may perceive themselves as having caused the death by not being a good enough child, or because they were naughty – 'Dad and I had a row the night before he died'. They may feel guilty for surviving, getting on with their life and having fun.

Anger

A child may feel angry towards the deceased for abandoning them and their family, for not being there in the future and at times when they may need them most. Anger may be directed at the living, perhaps the person perceived as causing the death or at another relative for not dying instead. Children feel angry at being excluded from what is going on, this may be the funeral, viewing the body or preparing a memorial. Parents often exclude children with the best possible motives. They wish to protect them and spare them any further anxiety. Adults may feel that a full explanation of the situation would be too confusing for the children. However these motives, whilst laudable, are misguided and often only serve to isolate and anger young people further. Sometimes the child's anger is less focused and is mainly because life has changed so dramatically that things will never be the same.

Confusion

Children often become easily confused by adults who struggle to find appropriate words to explain an event which is very complex, particularly in cases of murder or suicide. This sometimes leads the adults to give over-simplified accounts or explanations, creating gaps in the child's knowledge. This can lead to confusion over the actual circumstances of the death or the sequence of events. Young people can be confused about how to react particularly when they receive conflicting advice from well-meaning adults. Granny may be saying 'You have to be a big girl now, don't cry and try to help mummy as much as you can' and a teacher or friend might say 'It's OK to feel sad and cry, you let it all out'. The child then wonders just how they should behave as they have not yet learned (as adults usually have) that both behaviours can be appropriate depending on context and circumstances.

Fear and anxiety

When a death occurs we can sometimes become anxious about our own mortality, and children are no exception. They begin to fear for their own life and for others around them. They worry about becoming orphaned or losing other members of their family or friends. Children are often anxious about forgetting the deceased; what they looked like, the sound of their voice, their habits, and things they did together. There is fear about the future, the loss of security and constancy in their life. Where the death has been caused by murder they may fear the perpetrator is still out there and may come for them. If the death has been caused by an accident children may go on to develop fears about particular places; vehicles, fire, water and so on.

Helplessness

Children feel powerless to help the adults in their life through the grief. Often the only way they feel able to help is by being 'good', taking on a caring role or helping with chores. This can feed a child's denial of grief and of expression of feeling and may bring the additional burden of being more adult, thereby losing part of their childhood. They feel powerless to help themselves through grief as they struggle to understand their emotions and behaviours.

Relief

In the same way that adults often feel a sense of relief immediately after a death (particularly where there has been a long illness), so a child can also feel relieved when someone dies. However it is often more difficult for them to acknowledge and express this as it may provoke a 'shocked' response from adults and serve to sublimate the child's feelings into something more acceptable but less genuine. Relief may be more acutely felt where the relationship with the deceased was an ambivalent or abusive one. This may then be followed by a period of confusion as the child struggles to understand how to grieve for someone they loved but may also have hated or feared.

This is not a definitive account of children's feelings, behaviours or reactions or the reasons for them, but ones which have most often been expressed by children during their grief work. How children understand and react to death will always vary and will largely be affected by their age and developmental level. The following is a guide to understanding this a little better:

Age 0–2

The works of Bowlby and Erikson (Bowlby 1969, 1973, 1980; Erikson 1965) show how very young children can react to separation:

- They are able to search for the lost object and protest when the object does not appear: for example, a baby may throw a toy over the side of the pram and cry for it to be retrieved.
- At a later stage of development, the child will look over the pram for the object and may even try to retrieve it for themselves.

When a death occurs, particularly of a primary caregiver, the child will seek the presence of that person and experience a sense of loss. Erna Furman (1986) described a two-week-old baby as exhibiting protest behaviours such as crying in order to retrieve the lost person, refusing their food and experiencing a disruption in their bodily functions. Intellectually the child will not be able to understand the permanence of the loss and will expect the person to return.

Age 2–5

At this stage the young child has developed the capacity to think, reflect, inquire and have a degree of self-control. That gives him or her a greater degree of independence and an enhanced sense of self-esteem. Experiencing a death at this stage can undermine a child's self-confidence as their world becomes unreliable and insecure:

- They will cry, yearn and cling.
- In play they will often make attempts at reunion with the deceased person or act out death or their understanding of the facts.

Intellectually they try to make sense of the events, but they will often become easily confused by explanations. Their ability to retain information is still developing, therefore they will need to be told repeatedly about the loss. They will often believe that death remains reversible and so, for example, may wish to dig up the dead body to see if it is alive again.

Age 5–9

Having acquired the basic skills for social integration, the child finds itself in the wider social network of school. This may place demands on the grieving child in terms of other people's reactions and expectations. They may also have to cope with remarks from peers and others.

- They are learning who they can trust with their thoughts and feelings.
- They will watch adults' reactions to grief and will sometimes deny their own grief in order to protect an adult's feelings. Children may also take their cues from adults around them and copy reactions.
- They have a greater awareness of guilt and may feel they were responsible for the death by illogical reasoning such as, 'Daddy died in a car accident because I was naughty the night before'.

This is also the age of fear and fantasy and a child may personalise death as a skeleton, monster or ghost. Children become curious about the rituals surrounding death and about the functions of dead bodies, often asking such questions as whether dead people need food or clothing, or feel cold.

Age 9–12

Greater cognitive ability at this age gives the child an awareness of the finality of death: that it is common to all living things and that it is final, universal and inevitable. This can lead the child to a recognition of the possibility of his or her own death, which is a frightening concept. This can mean:

- There is a likelihood of psychosomatic symptoms being induced.
- These symptoms are an unconscious attempt by the child to draw attention to their distress.

The child is beginning to grieve in a more adult way and may often deny the sense of loss and try to 'get on with life'.

Adolescence

Adolescents are able to grieve more as adults do, with appropriate crying and with feelings of sadness, anger and depression. They may also have suicidal thoughts or may express intense emotion through other forms of self-harm.

- Adolescents have powerful emotions which may lead to them question their identity and the meaning of life. They often have a sense of impending doom and of a foreshortened life.

- In their questioning they may become interested in the occult, the afterlife, near-death experiences and the rites of different cultures in order to find meaning.

- They may indulge in risk-taking behaviour as life becomes 'cheap' or as a way of taking some control. Substance misuse may result as a way of escaping grief.

- Adolescents may reject adult values as life becomes more unpredictable. They may however go to the other extreme and question nothing becoming over compliant as they feel life has no meaning.

- Socially, there may be pressure upon them to take up more adult roles, particularly when a parent has died.

Peer group solidarity is important during adolescence as adult values and priorities are rejected. Grieving adolescents often have high expectations of support from their peers. Friends may be an important influence on the grieving process during adolescence, and there may be some members of the peer group who will not know how to react when one of their group experiences a bereavement, after all they themselves are going through the trauma of adolescence too. This can lead to the bereaved young person feeling that he or she has become isolated from their group and is an emotional stranger.

Conclusion

It must be stressed that these stages, emotions and behaviours are only intended as guidelines and children and young people may not fit neatly into the categories or exhibit exactly these signs of grief. To confuse us further, children may re-experience their grief as they get older and reach a new level of understanding. A bereavement in childhood may advance a child's understanding of death and its consequences. It may, therefore, happen that a child will exhibit features described as occurring at another stage in development, regardless of his or her age. They may show some or all of the signs of distress, or just to confuse us, none of them. It is also true that many of the signs recognised as grief may also be indicative of some other trauma in the child's life. Even if the child has been bereaved a further traumatic event may overlay the grief and need far more urgent attention. These guidelines are intended to help us look behind the presenting problems, to begin thinking about what might be troubling the child, so that we can formulate ideas about how we might help them.

Key Points

- Children experience the same range of emotions as adults.
- Children are often unable to verbalise emotions and may express feelings through their behaviour.
- Children have different levels of understanding and reactions at different ages and stages of development.
- Children 0–2 will experience a sense of loss but will not understand the permanence of that loss.
- Between the ages of 2 and 5 children will have a greater understanding of the concept of death, but will be easily confused by explanations.

- Between the ages of 5 and 9 children become more curious about death and the rituals surrounding it. They are also more aware of other people's responses.

- Children aged 9–12 understand the finality of death and may become frightened by the possibility of their own death.

- Adolescents grieve more as adults; they have powerful emotions which may have a considerable effect of them.

- Children may exhibit feelings typical of a different stage of development. They may re-experience their grief as they enter a new stage of development.

CHAPTER 2

Traumatic Bereavement

Any bereavement in childhood could be described as traumatic but, without underestimating the importance of bereavement for children, I believe a distinction is necessary between a bereavement which is stressful and one which is traumatic. A trauma is a powerful shock with long-lasting effects; being exposed to an overwhelming event which renders a person helpless in the face of danger. In bereavement terms this could mean an horrific encounter with death, for instance witnessing a suicide or murder, or the child being in the same accident where a death occurs.

A child's grief may be inhibited by the nature and impact of the traumatic event and the usual techniques used to help someone through grief become useless. The trauma itself may have to be dealt with before grief work can begin. There have been a number of studies and writings on children and their reactions to traumatic events (Black 1993; Furman 1986; Pynoos and Eth 1984; Pynoos 1992; Terr 1991), and in this chapter I will bring together some of the key issues from this writing which can help in trying to understand the traumatised child.

Memories and Grief

Short-term memory, which is our first perception of an event, is processed into long-term memory by adding meaning to the information which links to prior experience and beliefs. We can then recall at will. Memory revival is imperative in the process of grieving, allowing the bereaved to reminisce, ascribe feeling and later to internalise or accommodate the bereavement experience. Traumatic images may have to be processed before grief work can begin and this can make dealing with traumatic grief all the more difficult.

- The way a traumatic event is processed into memory differs from the way in which other stimuli are processed.
- This affects the recall of such memories. They may be experienced as 'flashbacks' and intrusive memories rather than being recalled voluntarily. This can be a very distressing and frightening experience for children.

The recalling of traumatic events around death have to be handled very sensitively. Children and young people may try to avoid memories or reminders of the event in order to prevent 'flashbacks' to the horror of the last time they saw the deceased. If the child persists in blocking out the recall of this event or memories of the deceased, they could be suffering from post-traumatic stress disorder (PTSD).

PTSD in Children

It is possible to diagnose post-traumatic stress disorder in children if certain symptoms appear in a particular way and can be linked to a stressful bereavement or event. The diagnostic measure is called DSM-IV (Diagnostic and Statistical Manual of Mental Disorders – American Psychiatric Association) and is used by trained therapists to determine whether PTSD is present. The following is a summary of the criteria:

- The child has been exposed to an event where they witnessed actual or threatened death or serious injury. The child's response involves intense fear, helplessness or horror.

- The trauma is re-experienced by 'flashbacks'; recurrent dreams of the event or frightening dreams without recognisable content, suddenly feeling as if the trauma were recurring, repetitive play in which themes of the trauma occur.
- There is a diminished interest in activities; feelings of detachment from others; change in character, sense of foreshortened future, irritability, decreased concentration, difficulties in expression of feeling.
- Hyper-alertness is present; sleep disturbance; guilt about surviving; memory impairment; avoiding activities which recall the trauma; intensification of symptoms when exposed to similar events.

These symptoms must exist for at least 28 days before the diagnosis is made. This makes a distinction between stress reactions immediately after an event and illness likely to persist over a period of time. The symptoms are distressing, with images and memories of the event being imprinted on the brain which return unbidden to further frighten and disturb a child. However, it is possible to alleviate these fears with *expert* help enabling the child to continue their grief work and recover from their experience. If you believe a child may be suffering from PTSD, it is crucial to obtain an expert opinion. *Do not* try to continue working with the young person as this could cause further trauma.

Signs of Traumatic Reaction

Symptoms of traumatic grief are, in part, similar to ordinary signs of grief in children as described in Chapter 1. However there are some differences.

- Nightmares occurring soon after the event usually represent the trauma itself, later often becoming transformed into

more generalised dreams about monsters with elements of
their trauma appearing symbolically.

- Children may suffer from 'night terrors' which is a state that
  occurs in stage four sleep. The child will look as though
  they are awake and appear terrified. Their eyes will be open
  but they will not be able to see or recognise anything. They
  may be dreaming at this time but will not remember the
  content, however, they may play it out when awake.

- Children may appear to be in a state of paralysis of action or
  show an absence of feelings; they may appear emotionally
  numb. They may retreat into a state of apathy with a lack of
  interest in play and normal activities.

- Hyper-alertness may occur, where the child remains
  hyper-vigilant. They startle easily and experience fearful
  anxiousness which they apply to all areas of their life. They
  are constantly on the look out for threat and therefore
  energy is not available for being sad or grieving.

- Children may easily become aggressive as they misperceive
  normal situations as threatening their safety and integrity.

- Additional stress can be caused when the child is exposed to
  reminders of the event, for example going in a taxi, taking
  an escalator, going in a boat, seeing knives etc., this will of
  course depend on the circumstances of the original event.
  They may try hard to avoid such reminders.

- Children may also dissociate, that is disconnect themselves
  from their experience. This is evidenced by not feeling or
  experiencing pain. In this state children often recount their
  experiences as though they were a detached observer or may
  appear not to remember being there.

- Re-enactment of the event can occur particularly in younger
  children. There may be repetitive, unresolved play around
  traumatic themes, play which the child concentrates on but
  which gives him or her no pleasure. They may enact

dangerous parts of the event in order to master them and in older children this may manifest itself in antisocial behaviour. In situations where the trauma involved a crime, the young person may commit offences similar to those of the perpetrator.

- Children may have misperceptions of the duration and sequence of events and they may over elaborate details.

Age-appropriate Behaviours

As with other bereavement reactions outlined in Chapter 1, reactions in traumatised children are influenced by their developmental stage. These can be categorised as follows:

Pre-school

Children may become withdrawn, subdued or even mute. They show anxiety at being separated from their primary caregiver and become easily upset by changes in routine. Sleep pattern disturbances, nightmares, sleepwalking and regression to early patterns of behaviour are all common. In play or in the recounting of details children generally focus on, and repeat, the central action of the events, disregarding other details. The fact that they do not remember peripheral details may lead adults to assume that the child did not notice, or has forgotten, the central event.

School age

School-age children may show a greater diversity of change, appearing to be inconsistent in their behaviour. They may become irritable, rude or hostile. Conversely they may become passive and inhibited. New fears will emerge such as being in certain places, sensitivity at particular times of the day or feeling that parts of the house are 'scary'. Compared to younger children, they may complain more of illness; stomach pains or headaches for example. There will almost always be a decline in school performance. This may be due to the child becoming too aroused by the noise of normal school life (particularly shouting) to concentrate, or because at times when they are meant to be quiet and working alone, 'flashbacks' to the trauma intrude.

Adolescents

Adolescents reactions are very much like those of adults with PTSD. There may be an increase in rebellious and antisocial behaviour, including possible mis-use of drugs or alcohol to relieve the intrusiveness of the trauma. A loss of impulse control, which could threaten their life, is particularly worrying as adolescents have easier access to vehicles or weapons, such as knives. In their rage they may hurt themselves or others, damage property or commit other major crimes. They are also likely to be preoccupied with feelings of accountability, responsibility and revenge.

Emotional Issues

There are a number of emotional issues which affect children and young people following a traumatic bereavement which influence how they are helped.

- Where a number of children or young people were present at the traumatic event each of them will have different perceptions of the incident. Therefore there will be different recall triggers and intrusive recollections for each of them.

- They may be unaware of what others know or remember. They may fear for the safety of others if they have not seen them since the event. For these reasons it may be important for the children to meet with their peers following exposure to a traumatic death.

- Media intrusion may cause distress and anger as children are followed or hounded for information. Media interest may go on for a protracted period as new evidence or witnesses come to light or documentaries on the incident are made, for example the Fred West murders.

- Children who are required to appear in court to give evidence about the incident will experience further stress. Children need support around the court process; for example someone who can explain what will happen, take them to see the court, explain who is who etc.

- Police, coroners reports or court testimony may also reveal previously unknown information, re-exposing children to the event and possibly creating new intrusive memories or images.

- In cases of murder there may be issues surrounding the child's identification either with the deceased or with the perpetrator. This might involve their appearance, gender or behaviour.

These emotional issues can compound the trauma and magnify the child's reactions, increasing their sense of helplessness and confusion. Their affect and importance should not be underestimated and at times these issues may be in the forefront of the child's mind and need to be dealt with over and above the bereavement.

Parental Murder

Of all the traumatic bereavements, this must surely be the most horrible to deal with, particularly when the child is a witness to the killing. There is strong evidence from research carried out by Robert Pynoos *et al.* (1987) that children suffer prominent post-traumatic stress reactions when they witness death or injury. When the death is that of a parent there is little wonder they suffer. How can a child begin to reminisce about their dead parent when their last memory of them may be an image of mutilation or

the sound of their cries for help. Even if the child was not a witness to the event, they suffer in additional ways when one parent
kills another.

- Post-traumatic stress disorder is likely to be more severe and
  longer lasting when the death was the result of human
  action; for example when a parent kills a parent (Pynoos and
  Eth 1986).

- Adults find it particularly difficult to talk about violent
  death with children, sometimes giving misleading
  explanations or maintaining conspiracies of silence.

- Children often overhear information or see media coverage
  of the incident leaving them feeling they 'know what they
  are not supposed to know', but keep it secret (Bowlby
  1979).

- The stigma and shame attached to being the child of a
  murderer can prevent a child from talking about themselves,
  their situation or their fears and worries to others outside
  the immediate family. This silence further increases the
  likelihood of a complicated grief reaction.

- The child may also be suffering the stress of having
  previously witnessed numerous violent acts between the
  parents prior to the final fatal incident.

- The child may struggle with massive conflicts of loyalty
  between the dead parent and the accused parent. They
  effectively lose both parents in a single, sudden event as the
  accused parent will probably be arrested and held in
  custody.

- There is likely to be conflict within the extended family
  around issues of responsibility and blame. Previous
  incidents, sometimes relating to unfaithfulness between the
  couple, may be brought up in arguments amongst relatives,
  thereby exposing the child to previously unknown
  information about either parent.

- Even after the trauma has been dealt with, an impending court case may continue to prevent the child from beginning any grief work, since the outcome may be the loss of their surviving parent. For some children the need for 'justice to be done' may be overridden by their need to retain one parent.

One highly significant long-term issue is that of the child's identification. The child may identify themselves with the murdered parent, perhaps becoming passive and putting himself or herself in situations where they are at risk or become a victim. Alternatively the child may identify with the perpetrator, feeling that they too are bad or have murderous feelings. Family members may also experience difficulty here, for example a child who behaves aggressively (which they are likely to do after an experience of this kind), may become labelled as being 'Just like their father, they'll turn out bad too'. These feelings in extended families often lead to the child being prevented from seeing the accused parent whilst she or he is in prison, as a way of protecting them either from exposure to a 'bad' influence or from the pain of the situation in general. However it may be helpful for the child to see the accused for the following reasons.

- They may need to redress their last experience of the parent by seeing them in a calm, safe situation in order to get a more balanced view of them.

- They need to address issues of fantasy versus reality; 'Is this man really a monster?' or 'Where is my Dad? Perhaps the police shot him too'.

- To hear an apology from the parent for the suffering they have caused the child.

- To learn more about the nature of the parents' relationship together and whether there had been good times and feelings of love for each other.

- To begin to address issues of identification and self concept.

Even though these points may need to be addressed, a professional assessment of the situation is important to determine whether or not it would be helpful to the child for them to see the accused at this time. If a decision is taken to go ahead with this course of action a considerable amount of preparation for the child is needed.

Conclusion

Where possible, a child should be given the opportunity to talk as soon after the traumatic event as is practicable as there are often 'windows of opportunity' where work can be done. If the opportunity is missed, emotional blocking may inhibit later work, sealing in the horror of the event. Other opportunities may occur at other times of stress or trauma in the child's life, doubling their distress. All children involved in a traumatic bereavement, no matter how this occurs, need prompt, careful and skilled intervention.

Key Points

- There is a distinction between a bereavement which is stressful and one which is traumatic.
- The brain processes traumatic events in a different way from other stimuli.
- The traumatic event may need to be dealt with first before grief work can begin.
- Post-traumatic stress disorder may be present and should be diagnosed and treated *by trained professionals.* The symptoms are specific, distressing and intrusive and will cause further stress if not attended to.
- Symptoms may be concealed from family and friends; professional help is essential to identify whether or not the child is suffering from PTSD.

- Traumatised children's behaviour can be categorised into pre-school, school age and adolescent, with specific features in each category.
- Additional emotional issues such as media intrusion or court proceedings may add extra stress to children and young people.
- Parental murder is an exceptionally difficult traumatic bereavement. Issues of blame, loyalty, identification and stigma may increase a child's sense of isolation and add to distress.
- In parent on parent murder it may be beneficial for the child to see the accused parent whilst in prison to begin to address vital issues. This should only be undertaken following an assessment and adequate preparation.

CHAPTER 3

Secondary Losses in Bereavement

When a family member dies, not only do children have to cope with the loss of the person and their special relationship, they often have a series of secondary losses to consider, some of which often do not come to light until well after the initial impact of the loss occurs. These secondary losses tend to compound grief and when they occur later in the period of mourning, often go unacknowledged as having an effect on the child. The following flow charts and information help to show how one loss often has others following in its wake.

Death of a Parent

Figure 3.1 charts the secondary losses when a parent of a two-parent family dies.

Income

With the death of a parent there is often a loss of income. A working parent whose partner dies may find themselves struggling with the decision to give up work in order to care for their children. A change in status for the parent connected to loss of earnings, can have an important influence on the child's grief. How ones' community, and indeed society generally, view people on a

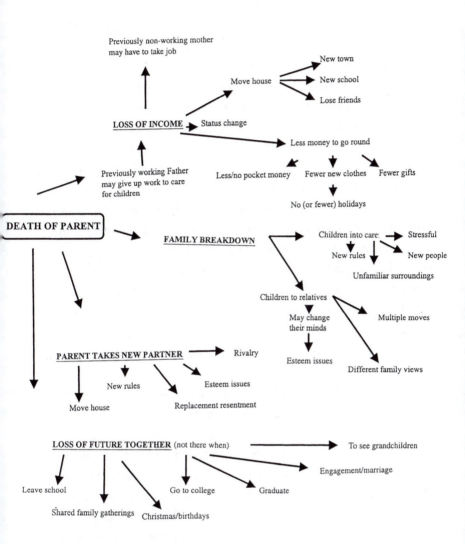

Figure 3.1 Secondary effects of childhood bereavement

low income or on benefit can have an effect on grief. The way one feels about one's self, for some, may be derived from the job they do or the income they earn and when this goes so can self-confidence and self-esteem, adding to the depression already associated with grief. Stress can also be produced when a previously non-working parent has to take a job to provide an income to raise his or her children. This can add stress to both the parent and the children as some of the knock-on effects like disrupted meal times, child-minding, less time to spend with the children etc., start to take a toll.

The bereavement may also mean moving house which is not only stressful in itself but has its own attendant losses. Everyone has to get used to new surroundings; a new town or city, possibly new schools and new friends. Then there are the issues of memories associated with the old home. Some bereaved people move house to try to escape the memories of their loved one only to find they follow them. Those who resist an inevitable move fear this loss of memories and often do not believe they carry their memories with them.

Another financial effect, but one that is not always thought about, is the possibility of much more money being available to the grieving family. Sometimes the deceased is heavily insured to make sure his or her loved ones are provided for after their death. For the bereaved family the income from this insurance may save them hardship, but it may also bring its share of troubles. People can feel guilty at profiting from someone's death, causing them much anguish when it comes to using the money to support themselves. For others the money may bring on a spending spree; pursuing all sorts of dreams in order to try to evade the pain of their grief. For children, the increase in disposable income in their family may be the beginning of a danger period as the grieving parent tries to compensate for the child's loss with material goods thus also providing the child with a way to avoid their grief too.

Family changes

In some extreme cases the death of a parent could lead to the children being taken into care. Perhaps where a mother or father can no longer cope with taking care of their children; where they relied heavy on the deceased to keep the family together, the last resort may be reception into care. It may also happen in the case of both parents dying at the same time or within a short time of one another. Initially other relatives may step in to help or even agree to take the children into their own families. Sometimes this is successful but in some cases, after only a short time, this arrangement can break down and may eventually result in social services offering accommodation. Relatives mean well, they have the best possible motives and the children's interests at heart, but they are not always fully prepared for the child's level of grief, or they have not really appreciated the complexities of bringing someone else's child into their home. Likewise the child may find it difficult to cope with their grief on top of the new regime of living with others, one issue compounds the other and eventually the child may find themselves pushing at boundaries, or at worst, rejecting their foster family. Reception into care as the result of a death in the family is rare, but other changes in family make-up are more common. Sometimes extended family members step in to help the bereaved parent care for children. However, this can change the dynamics in the family as the nature of adult relationships change, and this may be just as difficult for children to accommodate.

Mum or dad may take a new partner which will undoubtedly raise many issues for both parents and children. Adults can find grief hard to bear, the gap created in their life when a partners dies can seem like a bottomless chasm. Sometimes the bereaved person takes a new partner quite quickly after a bereavement in order to fill the gaps left by the deceased; parent, provider, supporter, lover etc. For children this can be very difficult to deal with and raises many issues which generally do not come into the open but are apparent by the child's behaviour or attitude towards the step-parent. A new partner may bring new rules, there may be issues about a change in the balance of power and this can cause resentment. A child can find itself competing for mum or dad's attention or even their love as the two adults try to conduct their courtship within the existing family structure. A child's self-esteem and sense of belonging can be severely damaged in extreme cases, going on to create difficulties in future relationships if these issues are not dealt with.

Loss of future

When a parent dies, children fear losing their memories of times spent together and of milestones in their relationship. They also grieve for the loss of the future with the deceased. Their parent will not be there at important phases in their life to share good times, successes, failures, lend support and help them. Shared family gatherings will always have a gap, and the ghost of a dead parent can be very powerful at these times. Birthdays, anniversaries and Christmas will go unmarked by the deceased; the gap on the mantelpiece where their card would have stood is very poignant. When a young child is bereaved of a parent, they can almost be grieving for the rest of their life as they pass through all of their developmental phases. Whilst this will not always be active grief, and will not be as acute as years go on, a parent holds a special place in a child's life which cannot easily be filled.

Death of a Lone Parent

Whilst many of the issues raised with a death of this kind are the same as those from a two parent family, there are some special issues which should not be overlooked (see Figure. 3.2).

Reception into care

With the death of a lone parent where the second parent is absent, unknown or unwilling to take on the bereaved child, there is a higher probability of reception into care, generally leading to adoption, depending on the age of the child. This has issues related to identity, history and living in new surroundings, but it may also raise esteem and rejection issues concerning the absent parent. The child may begin to ask themselves, 'Why didn't they want me?' 'Who is my mother anyway?', and in some cases, 'Why didn't mum tell me about him, now I'll never be able to find out'. These are questions which the child will be trying to work through whilst coping with the early stages of their grief which could lead to depression or acting out feelings of rejection.

Change to absent parent

It may be possible for the bereaved child to live with their other parent although this arrangement can sometimes raise as many problems as it solves. The previously absent parent may have a new relationship and possibly more children, creating a separate family into which the bereaved child suddenly has to fit. There may be a certain reluctance on the new family's part to consider taking the bereaved child on and this may resurrect for the child previously unresolved issues relating to rejection or abandonment. The bereaved child themselves may want to reject the caring overtures made by the new family causing anger and frustration as they attempt to 'do the right thing' to help the child.

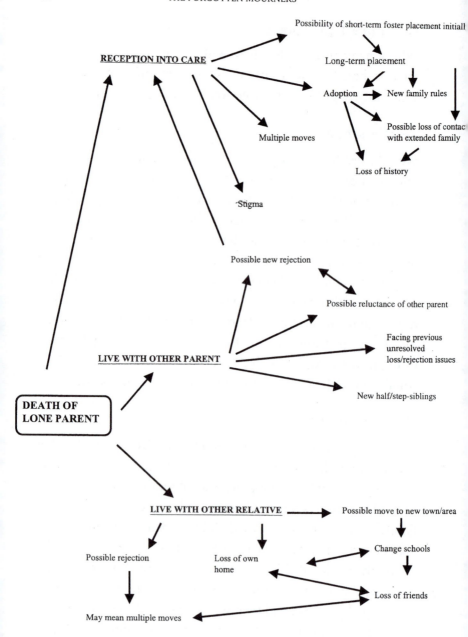

Figure 3.2 Secondary effects of childhood bereavement

It may force them all to re-evaluate their relationships as they learn to live together, perhaps for the first time. When her father died very suddenly, one adolescent girl found herself returning to live with her mother whom she had previously rejected. Mother and daughter faced dealing with their own separate and very different grief and the renegotiation of their relationship which had in the past been acrimonious at times.

Living with other relatives

When a lone parent dies other relatives may step in and offer to take the bereaved child into their home. This could be a grandmother, aunt, uncle or a more distant relation. Many of the same issues relating to the loss of familiarity, their home, school and friends exist with this kind of change in circumstances but there is one issue which seems particular to this sort of arrangement. When a relative takes on a child from within their own family they often do not consider there may be a mismatch and the child may not settle or feel comfortable. After all they are the same family, aren't they? Extended family members do not always fit together easily. Different lifestyles, values and priorities may get in the way of relationships being formed or consolidated, only adding to the child's grief and sense of isolation. Relationships may break down completely, and to avoid the prospect of the child going into care, they could 'begin the rounds', with one branch of the family after the other taking the child in and attempting to forge relationships. One child, who became particularly disturbed after the death of his mother, experienced just such a problem. He went with his older sister from one part of the family to the other until, in desperation, the family finally asked social services to help with care. Whilst one can understand the caring atti-

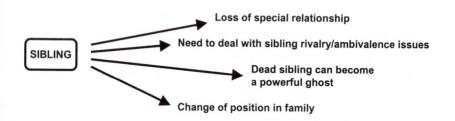

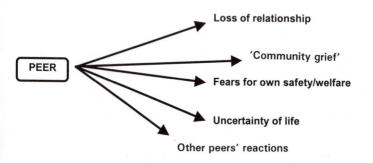

Figure 3.3 Secondary effects of childhood bereavement

tude first expressed by families, they may be unprepared for the complexity of the situation and its consequences.

Effects on Other Close Relationships

When there is a death of someone to whom a child or young person is close, the support and help the child receives may be focusing on their emotional needs. However, other issues relating to this type of bereavement may go unnoticed. Figure 3.3 shows additional losses associated with bereavement of this kind.

Extended family member

With the death of a family member such as a grandparent, aunt or uncle, some of the same issues relating to loss of future can occur particularly when the relationship was very close or where they were very involved. The deceased will not be there to share important times, they cannot now provide the kind of back-up support their role entailed (for example a grandparent), and children often feel different or left out as a result. The death of a close relative can also have a profound effect on the parent of the grieving child. When the parent's own parent dies, particularly if this is unexpected, traumatic or untimely, they are grieving their own loss and again the child can be forgotten. The parent's grief may increase the stress on the child as he or she tries to comfort, support or even care for their parent. The deceased may even have been a carer in the grieving family; perhaps if there is a disability. This death will have created a gap which may now have to be filled with help from an outsider which again may effect family dynamics creating new resentments, replacement issues and new stresses for everyone.

Death of a sibling

A dead sibling can be a powerful ghost in a family. There are almost insoluble issues raised when a child dies; the untimely nature, a parent's guilt at not being able to save their child, anger and frustration at young life never reaching its potential. These can all impinge upon the way a family deals with their grief and accommodates the change in structure created by the death. For the child, their status and position in the family may change as a result of the death. For example, they may move from being the youngest to being the oldest. Parents may now treat their remaining child as if they were an only child, lavishing the dead child's share of love, affection and material possessions on to them.

A grieving sibling has to deal with the loss of the special relationship that siblings have, even if this included fighting and squabbles. The death cheats the remaining child of opportunities to work through issues of sibling rivalry, competition, position and status, all of which help to shape future close relationships. The death of a twin brings special complications concerning separation and identity for both the parents and the remaining child.

Death of a peer

The death of a peer in childhood can have far reaching consequences for the grieving child. It is with the death of someone close who is of a similar age that adults begin to worry about the length and quality of their own lives. This is also the case for children. They begin to question how long they may live and whether they can escape the same fate as their friend. Some of the certainty and security of their childhood disappears when something as tragic and frightening as the death of someone their own age happens. Sometimes a kind of 'community grief' occurs where all those around the deceased are caught up in the event regardless of the closeness or depth of the relationship. When one of the school pupils of a local village was tragically killed in a road accident, almost everyone in the school and the village were caught up in the grief which enveloped them, and the child's family. Little provision was made to support the other school pupils through the experiences and a sort of 'grief hysteria' ensued provoking many and varied points of view from the adults involved on how this should be dealt with.

For the child most closely involved when a member of their peer group dies, they can often be trying to cope with their own grief as well as that of their friends, whilst their parents may not quite understand the effect this is having on their son or daughter. Children can feel very alone and unsupported at this time particularly if their school are also unable to deal with the issues.

Conclusion

I do not advocate that a child will face all or even any of these issues, some children cope remarkably well with the additional issues and become adjusted without too many difficulties. However, we should be aware these issues could exist and may become a problem. We should always look behind what we first encounter so that we do not miss the opportunity to help a child to express their needs.

Key Points

- Children need help to deal with secondary losses, such as house moves or change of schools.
- Financial loss or gain could create extra stresses for both parent and child.
- The death of a parent could result in family breakdown or reception into care.

- Arrangements to care for bereaved children by extended family may breakdown if there is inadequate preparation.

- Bereaved parents taking a new partner may bring issues of rivalry and replacement to the surface.

- A child will grieve for the loss of the future with the deceased.

- The death of a peer may leave children feeling anxious about their own health and longevity.

- Children need support from everyone around them.

CHAPTER 4

What Do Children Need?

The reason this book is called *The Forgotten Mourners* is because experience showed that was what happened to children who were bereaved. As adults got caught up in their own grief and the practical details of dealing with a death, children were forgotten and their needs went largely unheeded. In many cases it seemed as though the adults felt that children did not have needs. This is changing now as it has been recognised that everyone has individual needs when grieving, and children are no exception. This chapter will highlight some of these needs.

Information

Children need to have information as soon as possible after the death has occurred. During delays there are too many opportunities for children to create their own fears, fantasies and worries about *what* has happened and *how* it happened. Delays may also mean the child hears about the death 'accidentally' from someone else, and the chances of overhearing inappropriate adult conversations also increase. 'Overhearing' generally means only picking up snatches of conversation or things out of context. This creates 'myths' which can become set in the child's mind and then take a lot of dispelling. Bad news always travels fast and there will always be someone outside those immediately involved who will want to talk about what has happened. This person may not have all the facts or may even have malicious intentions and this makes the child very vulnerable.

The media can also play a part in providing inappropriate opportunities for children to get information. One young girl believed that was how she discovered her sister had been murdered. She remembered hearing it on the television news, and, as she perceived it, this had been the source of her discovery about the horrific event. It left her feeling hurt that, as she saw it, her family could not be bothered to tell her themselves. When the death has been as a result of murder, suicide or multiple accident it is newsworthy and before people know where they are they may be faced with a barrage of press reporters or even TV cameras. Events can happen so fast that those closely involved are not always aware of precisely what is happening. They may be caught off guard and suddenly find themselves saying something to a reporter that later they may regret. After traumatic events like these, parents and their children may become separated for long periods and may even have to live apart for a while. This can leave children at risk of scrutiny from the press and outsiders at a time when they are not able to rely on the security of their family network. Information released by the media may not always be factually correct and may have been elaborated in order to make interesting news. This could leave the child open to receiving misinformation and they may also be vulnerable to reporters' attempts at obtaining the 'human interest' angle. The child may be interviewed and asked distressing questions, or 'pumped' for information which may leave him or her feeling confused and frightened. This can undermine a child's confidence and may complicate their grieving process. They lack people they can trust, a safe environment within which to explore their feelings and reliable information to base their feelings on. Not only are they dealing with their own grief, shock and outrage, they may also be taking onboard that of the general public.

Explanations

Information given to children and young people concerning the death should be truthful and honest. This can be quite hard for adults as they fear they may upset or shock children unnecessarily by giving information, which to them, appears brutal in its honesty. However, if children are not told the truth they are likely to make up their own explanations in an attempt to understand what has happened. Sometimes children's fantasies can be worse than the reality and cause them more upset than hearing a frank and open explanation in the first place. Children can feel as if their life is out of control when something as traumatic as a death occurs, and if they have no access to information and sensitive help this feeling can become intensified. As pointed out in Chapter 1, one way for a child to control a situation is to apportion blame and sometimes it is all too easy for a child to blame themselves. Lack of explanations may lead to children having excessive problems with guilt and this can have an effect on their ability to progress through the bereavement process. Remember:

- Children's questions need to answered as honestly as possible.
- Be prepared to admit you don't know some of the answers rather than be tempted to make them up.
- A child can be helped to accept that not everything can be explained or fully understood.
- Do not spend *too long* explaining, children can't concentrate and will not take it all in. Make it short, clear and understandable.

- If information is given sensitively and honestly, children find situations easier to deal with, whereas 'protection' from information can lead to confusion and fear.

Adults should also avoid using euphemisms at all costs, even though they are often easy ways to get difficult concepts across, particularly to very young children. However they can cause more confusion and distress. 'Granny has gone for a long sleep and will never wake up', can have a devastating effect on a child. Explanations of this kind may result in the child having sleep disturbances, nightmares and fear of the dark which may take a long time to conquer. It is easy for an adult to use the metaphor of sleep when trying to explain death, but it is a difficult one for a child to interpret as sleep is a very big part of their lives and never waking again is very difficult and disturbing for them to contemplate. The use of the word 'lost' can leave children confused and may cause them to believe their relative is still out there somewhere and may indeed be 'found' again. Similarly, 'passed on' can lead to further awkward questions adults may not have prepared themselves for; passed on to what or where? If it has not previously been part of the family's culture, the concept of an afterlife can also be difficult for young children to understand, especially at a time when all sorts of other things are suddenly happening.

Try not to burden children with too many new ideas all at once. The 'drip feed' system works very well giving time in between for children to evaluate and assimilate the information they have received. It also helps if you do not use ambiguous remarks which a child can misinterpret.

- Be clear and understandable.
- Give information in a way which empowers children to return and ask you more.
- Tell the truth but be sensitive.

Help with Expressing Feelings

Children learn how to grieve from the way the adults around them deal with their own grief: for example, they will see whether it is acceptable to cry openly or not. They may ask themselves questions such as 'Is it OK to feel angry when I miss Daddy?' particularly if there is little or no expression of anger coming from other grieving adults around them. If adults explain their feelings to children, children will learn what is healthy and acceptable, but if feelings are ignored or suppressed children will get the message that to express them is wrong.

Children may need to act out; they may behave differently, get angry or aggressive, they may become withdrawn and quiet. All of these behaviours (as mentioned in Chapter 1), are part of the child's attempt to work through their grief, and should be encouraged in a sensitive and constructive way. If children repress their grief, there may be a tendency for problems or feelings to be expressed inappropriately or to be misplaced on to others. Angry and destructive behaviour shown by one boy at school was found to be rooted in his feelings towards the person who it was felt had been responsible for his brother's accidental death. The bereaved boy had not previously had the opportunity to explore the connections between his feelings and his behaviour. He was unaware that the angry outbursts towards teachers and peers were really about the anger he felt towards the person involved in the accident, and about his guilt for not saving his brother from death.

Children may also repress their grief and feelings when faced with the contradictions of other people's opinions about the way they should behave. Sometimes harm can be caused when well-meaning adults tell children they have to 'Be grown up now and take care of mummy/daddy'. It is a comment which is meant to bolster feelings of importance in the child but it can force the child to take on a far more adult role than they are prepared for. Behaviour often changes in these circumstances as the child struggles with adult responsibilities. It can rob a child of the relatively carefree days of their childhood as they find themselves worrying about bills, household chores, mum or dad's health and happiness and caring for younger siblings. Children should be included and encouraged to help around the house but they should not be expected to take on too many adult responsibilities. It is a question of balance; enough to make them feel part of the family which is pulling together, but not enough to burden them.

Attendance at Funerals

It used to be common to hear bereaved children say they had not been allowed to attend the funeral of a loved one. Neither had they viewed the body or had any part in how the funeral service was conducted. This is now changing and more children seem to be included in these rites of passage. However, at times it seems rather arbitrary and with little or no preparation and this can cause problems for grieving children.

Not being included may cause anger in the child about being left out. It may also create a gap in their knowledge and understanding about the process of death. For example: the last time a child saw their relative/friend may have been sometime ago, the person may have been well and healthy at that time. Suddenly the child is told the person has died, is being buried imminently (or has already been buried) and the next step may be the prospect of being taken to see the grave. How will this child understand how the deceased got to the grave? How that grave was created? Indeed, what is a grave? Whilst this example is somewhat exaggerated, it helps us to begin to see what exclusion could do. One child, whilst on a visit to a cemetery, asked others not to walk on the surface of the graves. She was worried they were walking on the dead people. She did not know that bodies were buried in a coffin or that they were at least six feet under ground. This shows us how worries, fears and confusions can be created for children. However they can be included and helped in sharing this important part of the grieving process.

Inclusion

Children can be made to feel part of what is going on by giving them clear and honest information and by providing them with numerous chances to ask questions. Explanations about what will happen next, are important to prevent gaps in knowledge. Asking the child what they would like to happen (even if this is not really possible to achieve), helps them come to terms with limits and boundaries both in life and after death. Also, allowing children to see adults grieving helps them understand the complexity of feelings and helps them to feel included in the family's grief.

Viewing the body

Whilst this is sometimes a rather daunting prospect, even for adults, viewing the body can help to dispel any myths created earlier on that the person is still living. Preparation and sensitive handling are the keys to this being a success. The child needs to know what smells, sounds and other sights the funeral director's rooms will hold for them. Whether there will be music, whether there will photographs of the deceased person on display, who else will be there, whether there will be flowers etc. They need to know that the body will be in a coffin and what that will look like, how it was chosen and why they are used. The child needs to know what the body will look like; whether there will be scars and why, that the body will not be breathing and will feel cold to the touch. There may be other questions particular to that child and their deceased, i.e. 'Will granddad have his teeth in?', 'Will James still have all the tubes attached to him?' It helps if someone has already visited the funeral rooms in order to be well informed about some of these issues. Time needs to be taken to anticipate some questions so that information may be gathered in order to give appropriate answers.

It is only after the child has all this information that they should be asked to make a decision as to whether they see the deceased or not. They also need to know this is one of the last opportunities they may have in order to say their goodbyes. Only in this way can the child fully understand the significance and importance of this rite. However, children should never be persuaded or coerced into seeing the body. Adults should try to make sure that the child has not agreed just to please someone.

Attending the funeral

As with viewing the body, children need to be given information before they decide whether they should attend the funeral. They need to know whether it is to be a burial or a cremation and what these actually entail. They should know the process of a funeral service, what it might include and whether they would like to say something about the deceased. They need to know about hearses, flowers and what tasks the funeral director's personnel will be carrying out. It is important to prepare the child for what takes place after the actual service. If it is to be a burial, they need to know about what happens at the graveside, and indeed what the grave site will look like – suddenly seeing such a deep hole may be frightening. Equally an explanation about cremation is important as the child needs to understand the body will not feel being burnt.

It is also important for the child to understand and take part in the post-funeral gathering, if there is to be one. Although these can sometimes be melancholy affairs, they are also opportunities for everyone to talk about the deceased as they knew them and the child may learn new aspects of the deceased they had not previously known about. It is important for the child to feel they can talk openly about the deceased and it is during this time it is most likely to occur. It is good to talk about things that would have made the deceased laugh or made them feel unhappy and to remember both happy and sad times they spent with them.

The level of the child's involvement in these parts of the process will, naturally, be largely determined by the nature of their relationship with the deceased and their closeness to them. Some of this preparation may not be necessary if the relationship was distant or superficial, but information about the funeral is essential if the child is to attend. If, after all the preparation, a child makes the informed decision not to see the body or attend the funeral, they must be helped to feel this is OK and not some failure on their part, children often feel they have 'chickened out' if they choose not to involve themselves in this stage. If the nature of the relationship is such that the child and their family will not be attending the funeral, it is still an ideal opportunity to bring the subject of death and its rites and rituals into the open for discussion.

Reassurance

With all that may have occurred after a death, children need reassurance that the world as they knew it has not completely disintegrated. They still need boundaries and structure to their lives in order to feel safe and not become overwhelmed by the grief around them. Although family life may become disrupted, a stable enough atmosphere provides the safety necessary for children to examine their feelings.

- Children need time to explore the new environment in their family caused by the death.
- Returning to as near normal a routine as possible provides security and reliability in surroundings.

Children often fear for their safety and well-being wondering, 'Who will look after me now?' particularly when a parent has died. They also worry about their other parent dying and leaving them completely orphaned, or about their own death. Younger children do not have the ability to understand that death is not 'catching' and therefore unlikely to happen to everyone around them. A child's imagination is a very powerful thing and they may need particular reassurance that they did not cause the death, either through their actions or their thoughts.

Conclusion

It is apparent from all this information that bereaved children's needs are many and complex. Above all else, children and young people need support from everyone around them; their family, friends, school and professionals such as social workers, GPs and health visitors. They need time and sensitivity, particularly at the beginning of their grief; helping them to accommodate their feelings.

Key Points

- Children should be told about the death in simple language.
- Children should be told promptly of the bereavement.
- It is important to give truthful explanations of the facts surrounding a bereavement and honest answers to children's questions.

- Do not use euphemisms and try not to be ambiguous. Be clear and understandable.

- Children need to be involved in the grieving process as much as possible and helped to express their feelings.

- Children may need to act out; they may become withdrawn or aggressive.

- Children need help to face contradictions in the way people speak about death.

- Children need reassurance that their world has not disintegrated.

- Remember that children are vulnerable to the scrutiny of the press and outsiders and must be protected from intrusion.

CHAPTER 5

What Can Adults Do?

The previous chapters have helped to show that children suffer every bit as much as bereaved adults and have to face just as many issues and problems too. However it is still sometimes difficult for adults to identify when a child is grieving and to meet their needs. The adults in a bereaved child's life, whether they are parents, carers or professionals, all have a part to play in helping the child through grief and making life more bearable.

Acknowledge Children's Grief

It is important that a child's grief is acknowledge by adults very early on in the period of mourning. Even if the adult does not fully understand how or why the child is reacting as they are, some acceptance of their reactions will go a long way in enabling the child to openly grieve. It helps if very soon after an explanation of the death is given, the child is encouraged to spend time talking about how they are feeling. Giving them some very brief and simple examples of grief and how children might experience this, will also help them understand that what they are going through is normal. An acknowledgement that these feelings can sometimes feel overwhelming and frightening can help to decrease some of the child's anxieties about them.

Adults caring for bereaved children need to understand some of the key issues of childhood grief in order to help them respond more effectively. For example, they need to be aware that children may try to protect adults from their grief for fear of upsetting them, that children may suspend their grief in order to take up adult responsibilities and that older children may delay their grief if they have heavy commitments at school. It is also important that adults do not underestimate the effect of multiple events on grieving children, and some work may be necessary in order to limit these occurrences; for example, moving house and changing schools. It may help to refer again to the charts in Chapter 3 to get a clearer picture of the consequences of some of these changes.

Understand the Re-emergence of Grief

When a child has buried or denied their grief it may come to the surface at any time, sometimes many years later. An event such as reaching adolescence could act as the catalyst. Unfortunately this can have the effect of confusing adults, as they expect the young person to have 'got over' their grief. Adults are often surprised, and not a little overwhelmed by the fact that it has come back.

The re-emergence of grief is not confined to instances where grief has been denied, it may also happen in children who managed reasonably well with their grief at the time the death occurred. This is often due to developmental issues (as covered in Chapter 1). As children pass through each new stage in their development their intellectual capacity grows, so does their understanding of grief. Unresolved or new feelings about themselves, the deceased or the circumstances of the death may surface serving to recall the acute feelings of grief first encountered at the time of the death. As a child reaches the stage at which he or she fully understands the finality of death it may cause them to face the reality of the gap that the loss has caused in their life. This is particularly so were a parent has died. As the young person grows they have to face life without their mother or father there to share special moments; passing exams, going to university, leaving home or having children of their own.

Sometimes new information comes to light about the circumstances of the death. This may be where there was an horrific death such as murder or where someone has committed suicide. In order to spare the child's feelings they may not have been given the full facts of the death at the time and may now be facing, perhaps for the first time, the true nature of the event. The child may find themselves not only grieving for the agony the deceased may have suffered, but also for the change which might be brought about in their existing relationships since this new information has emerged. They may find themselves being angry at adults for not having told them the truth or for lying to them, and being anxious and confused at having their basic sense of trust in adults undermined. It is, therefore, important that adults limit the possibilities of precipitating the re-emergence of grief by sensitive handling of information in the first instance.

Answer Questions as they Surface

Explaining death, especially to very young children, is never easy. An appropriate beginning could be to talk about life spans, using plants, trees and animals as examples, then move on to human life. The explanation a child receives should correspond to their age and developmental level.

- It is advisable to find out what, if anything, the child has been told already or whether it is believed they may have overheard information. Start from where the child is, what they already know or understand may guide you in how you approach the subject.

- Simple, honest and straightforward answers are the most helpful. Use simple language appropriate to the child's age, avoid jargon or technical words unless they are followed by a simpler explanation.

- Children need to be told the truth but truth can sometimes be shocking so care needs to be taken in phrasing.

- Children do not need to know everything in one go. Protracted explanations can lead to confusion so give information in 'bite size' amounts. Return to the subject as often as is appropriate and empower the child to ask questions.

- Predict some questions the child might ask and have some answers ready. Knowledge of the way the child thinks helps in anticipating their questions.

- The information giver should prepare themselves before beginning. Think about what you intend to say, practise it if necessary. Try not to become flustered if it does not go the way you practised it. Try to stay calm as this helps to calm the child, making them more receptive to information.

- If the information giver is not a member of the family, he or she must be sure to check with the family about any specific religious beliefs or feelings about death and afterlife before speaking to the child.

Of paramount importance is that children are told the truth. If a child receives half-truths these can create fears and fantasies in their imagination which can be worse than the reality. One child was taken to the interment of her dead mother's ashes, having been excluded from the cremation service. She later asked the social worker how they shrunk her mothers body. Further work with this child revealed she did not know her mother's body had been cremated, she did not understand what cremation meant and she believed that the body had been shrunk to a miniature doll-like size to fit in to the urn.

It is also important not to invent stories in order to soften the impact of information. Some explanations seem beyond our ability to master, some just seem too brutal, but when we use euphemisms to assist us we can create illogical circumstances which create confusion. One very young child was told that daddy was now above the clouds, driving his bus. This led the child to have many concerns and questions about the *ability* of buses to be above the clouds!

Anticipate Behaviour Problems in Bereaved Children

Because children's worries and fears are often expressed through their behaviour, a death in the family could activate the question 'Who will be next?'. The anxiety of how much more their security and safety will be undermined may cause the child's behaviour to change. They may become over protective of adults, constantly checking their whereabouts and their schedules. They may become unnecessarily agitated or overwrought when adults do not return home on time. These fears can sometimes result in the child unconsciously manipulating situations in an attempt to limit the adult's activities and absences from home. They may simply whine and plead, leaving the adult feeling guilty and concerned. Adults need to understand this behaviour and what has occasioned it. They should try not to become exasperated and angry at the child's intervention, nor to become completely housebound as this will only feed the child's anxiety. A balance needs to be struck and sensitivity to the child's anxiety is the key. Their fears need to be acknowledged and explanations of how this is a normal reaction need to be given. This can sometimes be difficult if adults are caught up with their own grief and do not have the time or energy to cope with demanding children.

Sometimes the usual house rules, limitations and boundaries lapse. This may exacerbate the child's difficult behaviour, since they sense the 'norm' no longer applies. If no one is prepared to draw appropriate boundaries and limit out of control behaviour, this may add to feelings of insecurity the child may be experiencing. The child may think that if the adults can't cope with the situation then how can they, a child, possibly cope.

In some cases children's behaviour continues to deteriorate because no one has noticed their distress. Therefore the child unconsciously 'raise the stakes' until someone takes notice. If no one takes action when they are moody or sullen, they may go on to become aggressive. Small items of property or belongings may begin to go missing at home which could turn into stealing from friends or taking other peoples property at school. Antisocial behaviour can often escalate until it becomes so serious that it comes to the attention of someone outside the family. This behaviour is usually rooted in the child's need to get help with their feelings and deep-seated fears. If adults are able to understand and anticipate this behaviour the bereaved child may have their problems acknowledged and attended to sooner.

Include Children in the Mourning Process

As covered in Chapter 4, it is important for children to be included in all aspects of the process of mourning. As adults want to protect children they sometimes exclude them from these important steps in this process. Often it is the adults own fears they are trying to protect as *they* may fear attending the funeral or viewing the body, if they can spare their children the same trauma it can help to ease their own pain. Remember:

- Give children explanations which will help them make an informed decision about attending the funeral or viewing the body.

- Remember that exclusion can lead to children feeling angry and disregarded.
- Grief may be complicated or delayed if the child is unsure what has happened to the dead person or if the child has not had a chance to say goodbye.

Funerals can be a tense time for families, and the adults are understandably occupied with their own grief. If a child decides to attend the funeral, it helps if an adult who is known to them, but is not part of the immediate family, takes special responsibility for them. During the ceremony they can be ready to explain things to the child and answer any questions that may arise. Some families like to include children in other bereavement rituals, such as discussing with them the headstone to be placed on the grave or the plaque in the crematorium. Decisions on how the grave will look, whether a rose bush or flowers are to be planted or what words will be inscribed on stones and plaques are all ways to include children, especially those who felt they could not face the funeral. Finding a way to say goodbye is important.

Keep the Memory of the Person Alive

A child's ability to remember and recall the deceased over a period of time may be limited, therefore assistance with remembering the person may be necessary up to the time of adolescence. Mementoes of the deceased person are important, so try to set aside something that the child can keep or it may be appropriate for the child to choose something themselves from the deceased persons belongings. The deceased may already have thought of this and have bequeathed something to the child in their will. These possessions may seem insignificant or strange; a single earring or a blow-up toy, but may be very poignant reminders for the recipient.

Children may worry about forgetting what the deceased person looked like so it is helpful to give them a photograph or have some displayed around the home. Sometimes preparing an album for the child to keep can help as it can make the child feel especially included and they are able to turn to them at times of distress. Videos are a wonderful reminder of the person who has died as you can see just how they looked and sounded. However, the way the deceased is almost brought alive by the moving pictures can sometimes be too much for the bereaved to bear, particularly in the early days of grief. Don't be surprised if children (and grieving adults) don't want to watch videos to begin with, it may be something they come to when their pain is less acute.

When families are separated, obtaining mementoes from the other party can be difficult, but a photograph alone may be sufficient to help a child with recall and aid resolution. In divorced families, it is sometimes assumed that the impact of the death of the estranged parent is less severe on the children because they were not living together anyway. This is not the case. Sometimes the death can be more difficult to deal with as the child may be trying to cope with unresolved feelings associated with the separation on top of those brought about by the death. Where the relationship between the deceased and the bereaved child was ambivalent or in cases where the parent was abusive, the child no longer has the opportunity to address those issues once the person has died and this may complicate the process.

> *Remember.* Even if relationships have been difficult, it may still be important to the child to keep the memory of the deceased alive; don't pretend that the deceased never existed.

Special times, like anniversaries, birthdays and Christmas need to be acknowledged. Children may remember around the time of the anniversary of the death but may not have a completely accurate recall of dates. Their memory may be 'jogged' by other events around that time; school summer holiday starting or ending, the changing seasons or public holidays, like Easter may remind them they are near the time. Children may need to share their thoughts and feelings at these times, or to mark the occasion in some special way, such as taking flowers to the grave or lighting a candle. Early on in their grief, on birthdays and at Christmas, children may wish to buy a card or gift for the deceased. This is all part of their way of marking the loss and should be regarded as normal grieving. It is only when these practices continue for a protracted period of time that they could be seen as an indication of something more serious.

On the child's birthday or at Christmas, they will be missing the card and present usually given by the deceased. Remember to acknowledge this. Perhaps it would help to leave a space on the shelf where the card would have stood or wrap an extra present. The child may tell you themselves how they would like this to be handled.

Conclusion

There is much that adults can do to smooth a child's passage through grief. It is clear the issues are complex and there is a lot to be considered. It is important to remember that giving time, space and compassion to a bereaved child will work wonders, but they also need understanding. It is important to familiarise yourself with as many of the issues as possible in order to be prepared.

Key Points

- Adults must acknowledge children's grief.
- Children may try to protect adults from their grief.

- Children may suspend their mourning process; older children may delay their grief.

- Multiple changes in their circumstances may delay children's grief.

- Be prepared for the re-emergence of grief, especially if children have not been given all the facts at the time.

- Explain death as simply as possible, in manageable steps that children are able to take in. Be truthful.

- Treat children as normally as possible, but expect possible behavioural problems.

- Include children in the mourning process and allow them to choose which rituals they wish to be included in.

- Keep the memory of the deceased alive, especially at anniversaries.

CHAPTER 6

What Can Schools and Teachers Do?

Schools and teachers have a significant role to play in the life of a bereaved child. School is perhaps the only place in which a bereaved child feels safe enough (with trusted adults and friends) to begin to explore their grief. It is important, then, that teachers do all they can to support grieving children in their school. It is understandable that teachers feel they have enough to do simply dealing with fulfilling their teaching requirements for children, without having to deal with complicated emotional matters too. However, teachers are in a prime position to at least recognise the signs of grief in children in their care and alert others who can take on the additional tasks of helping. Knowing how a bereaved child might react whilst they are in school could help to ease their passage through the long journey of mourning.

Look Out for Changes in Behaviour

Some children see school as a haven of peace and normality in contrast to the trauma and upset at home. They may, therefore, act as if the bereavement had not occurred in an attempt to preserve at least one area of their life as 'normal'. This gives them the ability to have some control over the periods of time they spend actively grieving. As previously mentioned, children have short sadness spans and need times when they can return to their normal everyday activities. This allows them time to assimilate information, to think or to be relieved of thinking, about what has happened. Just like adults, children need a break from grief, sometimes simply to enable them to gather the strength to go on grieving.

Conversely, some children may find school is the place to express their feelings, so try to be alert to changes in the child's behaviour: whether the child becomes more withdrawn or aggressive, for example.

- Some children may be more vulnerable and anything will trigger tears.
- Mood swings may become more common and some children may present more illness (headaches, stomach aches, general 'not well' feelings).
- Depression is more easily recognisable in older children.
- Adolescents may have suicidal thoughts and some may make suicide attempts.

Adolescence is a particularly difficult time and a significant bereavement at this stage can make it even more so. They may already be questioning ideas about life and death, and life after death as part of their normal development. Then, suddenly, they are faced with death at close quarters and struggling with these issues is compounded by the sheer weight of grieving for the deceased. Adolescents are far more aware of the implications of the death for their family. They may be more easily drawn into dealing with problems associated with lower income levels, child-minding issues and family management, than younger children would be and this can create an additional burden. Adolescents often act out their struggles with entering the adult world, issues of responsibility and belonging, so it may not always be easy to distinguish behaviour which might be their reaction to bereavement, from normal adolescent behaviour. This can make it all the more difficult for teachers to help, particularly if this help is rejected.

Problems related specifically to school may emerge for all age groups. Grief can make it extremely difficult to concentrate on anything, so school work may suffer fairly quickly with pupils falling behind, ignoring work assignments or failing to produce homework. They may become daydreamers, thinking about the person who has died or worrying about other members of their family. They may become subject to sudden outburst of temper or crying as their grief overtakes their ability to control their emotions. Other children may react in quite the opposite manner by overworking and putting all their energies into school activities. They may be trying to avoid the pain of grief by diverting their attention away from experiencing emotions into achieving at school. It is often easier to study, read books, research projects and write homework, than to think and feel about the person who has died. This child needs just as much attention and help as the child who is acting out.

It is important to remember that all children will act differently. Where there are siblings attending the same school, or even in the same class, do not expect them to have the same or similar reactions. Each child is an individual and will have had a different and unique relationship with the deceased. Each child will experience situations differently and will have different perceptions about what has happened. Some children may need help to understand the reactions and needs of their brother or sister. Just because they are related it doesn't mean they can empathise with each other!

Sometimes a child's grief can be delayed and it could be months or even years before they show the impact that the death has had on them. Sometimes another life event, such as a new step-parent or reaching adolescence, is the catalyst for releasing delayed or unfinished grief. This may go unacknowledged by teachers if the child has moved on to a new class, or even a new school, where teachers are not aware this event occurred. The passage of time also makes us believe the child should have adjusted by now, be over it, but for some children their grief may only just be getting the chance to start.

Be Aware of Potential School Refusal

Bereaved children sometimes feel they cannot face school at all. They are not sure who knows in school, which teachers or pupils have been told about the bereavement, and they may be unsure of what reaction they will get when they turn up for school. A bereavement can change the status of a child in school. It can make them an object of curiosity, and they may become subjected to all sorts of questions from others. It can make them a complete pariah, someone to be feared lest they bring death with them! All this makes for a fearful new experience.

The bereaved child's peers may all react differently, being unsure of how to approach them. They may ignore the child and not mention the death, then the child is left wondering whether others have been told about what has happened and upset that their friends are not supporting them. However the child may also become overwhelmed with so many questions that they cannot cope. Bereaved children often find they are taunted because they are now 'different' and other pupils say unkind and hurtful remarks which, if left unchallenged by adults, could ultimately lead to the child refusing to attend school. Taunting by others can also lead to an increase in aggression from the bereaved child as they try to defend the deceased and themselves from remarks like 'I'm glad your mum died' or 'It's the best thing that ever happened to your family'. If undetected, this can have devastating effects on a child's ability to grieve openly for fear of being ridiculed by other children, so early detection and sensitive handling is important.

Create a Supportive Atmosphere

Teachers can help a bereaved child by creating a supportive atmosphere where they feel able to talk and share their story and their feelings openly. This can start long before the child returns to school by making sure staff and pupils have been briefed about what has occurred. Preparing the child's class for his or her return could prevent them being ignored or the unkind remarks I have already mentioned. The other pupils also have the chance to ask questions of the teacher they may be afraid of asking the bereaved child, and it provides the whole class with the opportunity to explore the issues of life, death, illness and feelings.

- Allow the bereaved child to cry or be angry, and encourage expression of feeling within the classroom.

- Bereavement is also a learning experience for the rest of the class: it can help them to understand that grief is normal and natural.

- The bereavement may provide the opportunity to widen a class' knowledge of the grieving and mourning processes of other cultures and religions.

Once the bereaved child has returned to school some allowances may need to be made for a while concerning their behaviour in class. There may be times when they need to go to a quiet place with someone if they are upset. Generally it is best to expect them to function as normally as possible, but they may not always be able to sustain this. Try not to separate them from the rest of their peer group with *too much* special attention. Bereaved children often fear they have become 'abnormal' and separation or special treatment may serve to increase this fear and the risk of being taunted for being teacher's pet. The child may also be asking themselves the questions 'Who am I now?' and 'Are we still a family?', so they need plenty of reassurance in class that they are still 'normal' and not 'different'.

As the passage of time elapses, it is very easy for teachers and pupils to expect a child to feel better, or 'be over it'. However a child may go on grieving for quite a protracted time (depending on their age and developmental stage), so be careful not to allow these feelings, or unhelpful remarks like, 'Well you still have your dad', to begin to slip into your conversations with the bereaved child. Be aware of the bereaved child's discomfort and sadness around special times, such as mother's or father's day, birthdays and at Christmas. Schools holidays can also be a problem. The child may not have their mother, father or other special person to care for them during the holidays now, and returning to school after the holidays may feel like having to face an ordeal all over again. A simple personal greeting on their return may be all they need to give them a lift.

Acknowledge the Death

It may be appropriate for the class or the whole school to acknowledge the deceased, for example if it were a pupil or a member of staff. There are a number of ways this might be done depending on the circumstances. There could be a memorial service in the school hall or chapel, or a special school assembly involving members of the class associated with the deceased. This occasion may also be used for commemorating the life and school achievements of the deceased. The teacher may feel it is more appropriate to hold a small simple 'service' in the classroom which could, for example, involve lighting candles and drawing pictures.

- Some schools have a memorial book into which the names of any deceased known to children are put.
- When a member of staff dies, a more lasting memorial like a clock, wall plaque, equipment or trophy might be bought as a significant reminder of the deceased person.

Planting trees or bushes around the school and holding a ceremony at the same time is always a useful way to mark the death of someone intimately involved in school life. It leaves a beautiful reminder for later pupils (who may not have known the deceased) to admire. Acknowledging a death in a pupil's family in this way may not be appropriate. However some acknowledgement from the school is an important factor in creating for the child an atmosphere of empathy and understanding. The child should be asked how they would like the bereavement to be marked. Perhaps it would be more appropriate for the bereaved child to simply spend some time talking about the deceased, if they are able, or for some of the class to talk about the person, if they knew them. The idea is to acknowledge the life and work of the deceased and to share memories, in much the same way as happens naturally at funeral gatherings. The young person needs to feel their grief and feelings have been noted and are as important to others, at times, as they are to themselves.

Create Links with Home

Contact with the bereaved child's family can help with understanding the child in school. The family's pattern of grieving may be effecting the child without it being immediately obvious to the school, only by talking with parents or carers can this come to light. Children learn to grieve from the adults around them; what seems to be acceptable or how not to behave. The family may be taking the 'stiff upper lip' attitude and not outwardly expressing their grief and the child may follow this mode of coping, making it difficult to encourage the child to be open at school. Other families may be overwhelmed by grief, and the child can feel 'lost' as all normal patterns of living are disrupted and family rules and normal boundaries disappear.

If it is a sibling who has died, the parents may be idolising the child's memory. This can cause problems for the bereaved child; the parents may not be able to let go in favour of the living child. The bereaved child may feel it has to live up to the expectations the parent had of the deceased sibling, and this can cause anger, jealousy, resentment and frustration. If the parents are stuck in this mode of grieving, be aware that the bereaved child's needs may be ignored and he or she may encounter difficulties in resolving his or her own grief.

Some bereaved families have already been divided by separation or divorce. The child may not only be coping with the bereavement, but with other unresolved feelings around the initial losses involved with the break up of the family. There may be many other changes in the home resulting from a separation which the family are only just learning to deal with when their loss is compounded by the death of the estranged mother or father. The charts in Chapter 3 may help in understanding additional losses.

Create a School Policy

The creation of a school policy can help to provide a framework for all school staff to deal with death and all its eventualities. Staff feel supported and less vulnerable when an action plan has been agreed well in advance of a situation arising, and a policy can also safeguard children at their most vulnerable time.

The policy could cover such issues as whom to tell, where a child can go when they are upset, and which teachers will be identified to support a child. It is important to select key people for this task as not all staff will feel they are suited to act as personal supporters. The policy should also cover the issue of what to do should the school be involved in a disaster (Shears 1995), as although it may only involve a few people, the vibrations may be felt throughout the school. The issue of staff training and ongoing support should be addressed. As with any other situation, people feel less vulnerable and work more effectively when they have knowledge of a subject and how to begin to deal with it. Local resources need to be identified and the information kept up to date. Names and addresses of counselling organisations and agencies who offer support should be included, as well as details of professionals with whom the school can consult should the need arise. Some guidelines on how to handle interviews with the media would also be useful; facing the newspapers, television cameras or radio reporters can be a daunting prospect. Knowing how much or how little information to give out or whether to give no comment can be a hard decision to make during a time of crisis, so planning ahead is essential.

It is helpful to decide what arrangements could be made to help support pupils who attend a funeral during school time. If pupils are to return to school immediately after a funeral they may need time and space to explore the impact of the event. This can be done on either an individual basis or for a group. Key staff should be identified to provide this service. It may also be helpful to set aside a room or the hall and to provide hot drinks or food. It can be quite a shock to attend an emotional farewell to someone and then be expected to fit straight back into school lessons.

Loss and death should be included as a subject on the school curriculum so that these events are seen as a natural – if different – part of life. The school library should be stocked with relevant books on the subject, not only those dealing with the facts, but story books addressing the subject of loss and death. It is sometimes easier for children to relate to other children or animals experiencing this situation, than it is to acknowledge that it is themselves who have these feelings. Although there is a resources list at the end of this book, it is not an exhaustive one. Your local authority library services department will be able to advise you of the latest appropriate books available.

Conclusion

The role of teachers and schools is of prime importance to bereaved children. You may prevent a child's grief from becoming prolonged or complicated by your early recognition and intervention, so never underestimate your influence on the situation. At the very least, you can provide a welcoming and accepting atmosphere for a child to explore their grief.

Key Points

- Schools and teachers have a significant role to play.
- Be aware of changes in behaviour and of different ways that children may express their grief.
- All children will react differently and it may be a considerable time before they show the impact of the death.
- Be aware of the responses of the bereaved child's peers, these may lead to school refusal.
- Create a supportive atmosphere in which the child can talk and share feelings.

- Acknowledging the death by some sort of memorial in school may be appropriate.

- Be aware of the child's need for privacy at times.

- Do not overcompensate with too much 'special' attention, this can make them feel different and can create jealousy amongst other pupils.

- Remember that special times such as mother's day can be painful for the child to deal with.

- Try to ensure the school library has a selection of appropriate books.

- Create and maintain links with home.

- Ensure that there is a school policy.

CHAPTER 7

What Can Social Workers Do?

Social workers do not always become involved with families or individuals because of bereavement, but often become involved in cases where bereavement may have been an issue in the past. It is possible that because of past unresolved loss a person becomes a client of social services, perhaps a teenager who finally becomes too much for parents to cope with. It is, therefore, important to be able to recognise and understand the complexity of bereavement and grief and its effects on people. There is much that social workers can do to support the bereaved and help them work through their pain.

Support the Bereaved Child

A bereavement in the family, especially the death of a parent, may bring about many changes for the children involved. The charts in Chapter 3 help to show some of these changes, their consequences and at which points social workers may become involved. Social workers may be asked to accommodate children, to deal with adoption or assess adult relatives wishing to become foster carers. It may be necessary for the child to move from living within the deceased's household to living with the other parent. This can happen where the young person's parents are separated or divorced. The new partner, wife or husband of the deceased may not be able to continue to look after the bereaved child or the child may wish to return to their other parent. Whilst on the surface this may seem to be the best decision, the change can raise many issues connected to self-esteem, belonging and the stability of their future.

It needs to be recognised that if major changes occur as a result of the bereavement, the child needs time to adjust to his or her new situation before being able to begin any real grief work. In these circumstances young people sometimes shut off their grief totally and become disconnected from their feelings in order to avoid any further pain. New surroundings or new family members may prevent a child from being themselves or from feeling comfortable and safe enough to let go of their emotions. Their grief may have to wait until they feel more secure. However, children do not always disconnect. Some may go on grieving and showing signs of distress but may not be in a position to actively *work* on their feelings. In these circumstances children need to be 'held' and to have their feelings acknowledged and, a certain tolerance is necessary in order for the child to begin to feel secure enough to be able to let go. It is at these times that social workers can:

- Help families understand the impact of bereavement on children and why they may be behaving differently.
- Explain to both the children and adults about different ways in which people react to bereavement.
- Provide some space and time for individual work with children, allowing them to tell their story and express their feelings.
- Be alert to the child's reaction to a bereavement and help parents, teachers and other adults to understand that

possible emotional and behavioural problems in the child may be linked to the grieving process.

Social workers may also become role models for adults when talking to children, perhaps in how to approach the subject of death, or what words to use. In this instance, social workers are in a prime position to enable adults to prevent future problems by handling the early days of bereavement with care and understanding.

Help and Support the Bereaved Family

After a death in the family there are often many practical arrangements to be made. As the family can still be very shocked and numb, someone who is known to them, but outside the family circle, can provide information, guidance and support at this time. Relationships built up during the period immediately before the death can be particularly helpful at this time. Hospice or hospital social workers can play a very vital part for families during periods of long illness or where it is known that the illness is terminal. They will know which resources are available to the family, which other agencies or organisations can help and how to access these.

Where social workers become involved soon after the death has occurred, they can help the bereaved family face the reality of the loss and prevent denial occurring by talking through the experience with them. They may need to become 'mediators', helping family members to recognise each other's needs and responding to them. Social workers also need to be alert to the family's grieving patterns and recognise when a family – or individual – is becoming 'stuck' and needs help to move on. It may be necessary at this time to suggest more specialist help and some work may need to be done in helping bereaved families to see that accepting this help is not a failure on their part.

- Some families may keep a room as a perpetual shrine to the dead person; although this may be a normal initial reaction to the bereavement, the family need help if it is still operating at this level many years later.

- Families may become obsessive about visiting the grave long after the person has died. Children can be caught up in this pattern and may need freeing from it as their level of grieving may be quite different.

In families where a child has died there may be fears that something will happen to the surviving children. Therefore parents can become over-protective. Sometimes the opposite can happen; surviving children are rejected or forgotten as the parents withdraw into their grief and idolise the dead child. Social workers may need to spend time with parents helping them to see how these reactions can affect their children. Some parents overcompensate with their living children, either in an effort to make up for the loss or to help lessen the impact of it. Sometimes parents swing from one mode of operation to another as their grief dictates and they become lost in a confusion of feelings. It is here that social workers can help families to look at their grief reactions, guilt, anger and rejections and can encourage the expression of feelings within family members.

A bereavement can sometimes highlight existing family problems. When there has been a death in the family it often requires family members to 'pull' together to deal with the event, but in families where there are existing problems this may not be possible. Communication can be especially difficult, since they are often all grieving in their own way and showing it at different times. Each member feels they are the only one feeling like this and they are unaware of others' needs. Some are unable to ask for the support they need from their family and as each one becomes entrenched in their own position, communication becomes increasingly difficult. Couples may find it particularly difficult, feeling that their partner does not understand them or does not care. Sometimes roles can instinctively become complementary, when one partner is falling apart the other becomes a little stronger and takes care of the rest of the family. However this can also become a bone of contention as one feels guilt or failure and resents the other's strength and resilience.

The children in the family can be drawn into these complex dynamics, often being expected to take sides with one or other parent, and grieve as they do. Sometimes the children just sit on the sidelines watching their parents relationship fall apart in the wake of grief, helpless to stop it and suffering twice over as they also lose their parents. Social workers can help the adults seek out and make use of bereavement or couple counselling services. They can also support the children through learning to understand the full impact the bereavement has had on their parents.

Support through Court Proceedings

When a bereavement has occurred there may be instances where the judicial system becomes involved. At these times social workers may have an obvious role to play in terms of providing court reports and giving evidence. However, they may also have a less obvious, but none the less important part to play. In cases where an accident has occurred or where there are suspicious circumstances surrounding the death, a coroners court may be involved. Social workers can help family members facing attendance at court as this prospect can often be overwhelming or confusing. The proceedings do not always occur immediately after the event, sometimes many months elapse. Attendance at court can catapult bereaved relatives (who may feel they are just beginning to cope with their grief), back into acute feelings of loss again. In some cases, the delay before the court proceedings begin may contribute to grief being delayed, and as the case comes to court it can precipitate the beginning of grief. Families need support at this time, particularly children who do not understand how the court works or why it is necessary. Social workers can help with explanations and in some cases with accompanying the bereaved, especially children, to court hearings.

As outlined in Chapter 2, in traumatic bereavement where a child may have been witness to the event, they may be required to give evidence to a court about what happened. In murder cases, children are particularly vulnerable and testifying on the witness stand may lead to further distress. In these circumstances social workers may be required to help a child through this experience providing them with preparation for the courtroom appearance.

Conclusion

It may be difficult for social work staff to determine whether or at which point they become involved in bereavement issues with children and families. It is rare that bereavement requires statutory involvement, but some intervention during the early stages may prevent a lot of intervention at a later stage. Even with minimal intervention, social workers can play an important part in helping families with their grief.

Key Points

- Social workers can support the child and help them understand bereavement and its impact on them and their family.
- Social workers can be role models for adults in how to talk to children about death and bereavement.
- Social workers can help the family face the reality of bereavement and help them through the process.

- Work on communication between family members may be necessary to prevent further family breakdown.

- Social workers can help families identify when to seek expert help and how to access these services.

- Social workers may need to provide advice and information on practical issues, resources and how to access them.

- Social workers should be alert to the family treating the child in a different way – either overcompensating or rejecting.

- Social workers may have a special role to play in helping a child or their family through court proceedings.

CHAPTER 8

Working with Bereaved Children

Not all bereaved children will need counselling, but quite a few will need some help, if only to begin to understand what has happened. For a vast number of children, all the help they need is available from their family and friends. However there are some children who will benefit from help from outside of the family. Just like adults, children often find it easier to talk to someone not directly involved in what has happened. It helps to have a listener who is not emotionally involved, and who will not break down in tears when painful memories are revived. This does not mean the family have failed to support their child, only that some extra support is needed, possibly for them all, in coming to terms with this difficult situation.

There will also be a number of children who need specialist help, perhaps where there are existing problems within the family or where the death is particularly traumatic; for example a murder or suicide. Here we look at what help might be available to children.

Family Work

Some might say this is the preferred method of helping a bereaved child, since they live in a family, and grief effects everyone in the family to a greater or lesser degree. A family has to learn how to deal with the bereavement, how to communicate their needs to each other, and how to build a new life without the deceased person. These tasks can prove difficult when trying to achieve them all at once.

A death can change the dynamics in a family by creating new roles and by undermining accepted patterns of behaviour. Previously, the mother may have been responsible for disciplining the children and after her death, father has to learn how to take on this role. This can change how his children perceive him, and more than certainly change their attitude towards him at times. Family members may begin to behave in ways that are least expected of them and this can confuse and anger others in the family. Time needs to be taken to examine what is happening and how these difficulties may be overcome.

Each family member will grieve at a different pace, and this may create conflict and misunderstanding. For example, one person may contain their expression of grief and withdraw, whilst another may be more expressive and open with their grieving. Each of them has individual needs which the other may not recognise, or may not see as a suitable way to deal with grief. This can lead to either of them feeling that their pain goes unnoticed, or to feeling unsupported by those they love. Parents who immerse themselves in their grief may not understand how their child cannot react in the same way. They worry the child is being callous and unfeeling by not expressing their grief all the time. Equally, children whose behaviour is such that parents no longer feel able to cope, can often be seen as 'having something wrong with them, being difficult', rather than simply trying to draw attention to their needs. Family work aims to:

- address the way the family functions;
- create understanding between family members;
- help families to progress through the stages of grief.

This method is particularly helpful for addressing issues which arise when a family is stuck at a particular stage of grief, for example keeping a room as a shrine after a protracted period. People working with families may need to help parents understand their children's behaviour and what children experience at different stages of their development.

Family sessions can also be used as a forum to discuss practical issues following a bereavement, for example how frequently they feel the need to visit the grave and how to include children in the mourning process. The family worker or therapist can act as a facilitator to help the family discuss these difficult topics and to ensure that each one is listened to and their needs met. The adult family members may also need help in understanding the source of their present pattern of functioning. Family therapy may enable each member to examine their own history of loss and their ways of coping with it.

Some families may not need to go as far as seeing a family therapist. However, they may benefit from sessions with a person trained in bereavement work who can help them begin to sort out some of the difficult issues.

Individual Work with Children

Family work is undoubtedly of great value, but individual work with children also has a significant role to play. As already mentioned, talking with someone outside of those directly involved, can have a therapeutic effect in a number of ways. Whilst adult members of the family may move on in their grief, a child may become stuck at a particular point, or with a particular issue, because of their developmental stage. Individual work gives the child an opportunity to work through grief at his or her own pace and level of understanding by using methods which correspond to the child's age: for example, play and painting can be used in situations where it is difficult for a child to verbalise their emotions.

A child sometimes needs to be given space and time away from the family to express very deep feelings which he or she believes may upset or confuse the adults. Children are also very curious and often want to ask questions which may shock adults, such as what happens to a dead body. Working on an individual basis with children also provides the forum for them to express their fears and fantasies, clear up confusions and come to terms with changes within the family.

Whilst individual work is invaluable, children should never be worked with in complete isolation. A time will come during work with a child when some issues will need to be brought up with the family so that they can all learn how to move on. Permission will need to be sought from the child to discuss these points with the parents or carers and a great deal of sensitivity will need to be used in bringing people together in this way.

Group Work with Children

Whilst family work and individual counselling are both valid means of helping bereaved children, these methods may not necessarily address some very important issues. The sense of isolation that a child often feels, or the lack of support they get from their peer group are important factors in helping children work through their grief. The main aim in group work is to create a space for children to share with others in a similar situation, thereby fostering a sense of mutual identity and decreasing isolation. This in turn, can help to stabilise relationships outside of the group. Children who are finding relationships at school difficult, perhaps because of taunting, can find the support they need within the group to deal with these situations when they arise in the playground. When relationships with parents or carers begin to falter because of differences in thinking, the group may be the place to share this issue and to find new ways of dealing with it. There are many subjects which can be tackled and many goals that can be achieved by using group work as opposed to individual or family work, for example:

- the alleviation of isolation;
- an increase of self-esteem;
- the giving of reassurance and support by others of the same age;
- reducing feelings of powerlessness;
- a decrease in feeling stigmatised.

A bereavement group offers children the chance to 'normalise' their situation; to mix with others who have had similar experiences so that they feel less isolated and 'different'. The child may be the only one in their class, their street or their circle of friends who has been bereaved, so they may be feeling that no one understands what it feels like to be in their shoes. Bringing children together in a group can provide a mutual aid system; sharing with others and providing opportunities to hear possible solutions and ideas.

If the group work method is to help a child through their grief it should attempt to achieve the following goals:

1. Help the child to express the effect the loss has had (expression of feelings).

2. Increase the child's sense of reality of the loss.

3. Provide an opportunity for them to voice fears and concerns.

4. Create opportunities for them to acquire knowledge.

5. Encourage a healthy withdrawal from the deceased.

6. Help them to readjust after the loss – to seek new relationships, to adapt to a new position or role in the family or to become accustomed to a substitute family.

Whilst a well-planned and run group will provide opportunities for these goals to be met, the group should never aspire to meet them all for every child who attends. Children must be allowed to grieve at their own pace and allowed to explore some of the different stages they will eventually go through if they are not yet ready to face them now. For example, it helps a child to know that resolution is possible even if they are not yet at that stage. In order to facilitate this, it helps if the group is structured to enable the exploration of the stages of grief and mourning:

- shock, numbness, disbelief;
- anger, guilt, denial;
- yearning, searching;
- acceptance.

Planning a Bereavement Group

A detailed description of the planning of a structured group for bereaved children can be found elsewhere (Smith and Pennells 1993). However it is important to outline here what needs to be considered when thinking about running a group.

Embarking on a bereavement group should never be taken lightly. Although a very rewarding way to work with bereaved children, it is very time consuming. A great deal of effort has to go into the planning and preparation for groups and time also needs to be set aside for follow-up work. Therefore, one should make sure, before beginning a piece of work of this nature, that there is sufficient time and space in one's workload to accommodate the project.

There are several areas of planning which need to be considered before beginning a group, some of which will be entirely dependant upon the client group or community with whom the work is being undertaken; for example referrals taken from isolated rural areas. The method by which referrals are dealt is also important; will there be assessments and how will the paperwork be dealt with?

Other important considerations are the content of the programme, the number of sessions to be held, the venue and transportation. You may decide you need materials – books, paper, paints – or play equipment. The sessions should include drinks and some food (perhaps biscuits or cakes), providing a symbol of sharing and enabling the children to settle down and begin the work. The content of each session should be as varied as possible to avoid boredom. However, do not 'overfill' the session as this may result in tasks remaining uncompleted. Use techniques the children are familiar with, such as play, painting, working with clay, dressing-up or acting. Some time for free activity should also be built in to allow children to 'let off steam', and remember that adolescents also like to let off steam and may want to regress to simple contact games to do this.

Endings in a group of this kind are very important, so planning the ending as soon as possible is crucial. Have a party, go out for a meal or use the local amenities such as swimming, bowling or skating. Including the children in this planning gives them some control and helps them realise that not all endings are unpredictable or sad.

Not least of all, consideration has to be given to how the group will be funded. Simply buying refreshments will incur cost, without equipment, venue or outing expenses. Likely sources for funding will need to be explored before the detailed planning can begin and thought should also be given as to how much involvement funders will have in the project.

Conclusion

Working with bereaved children can be rewarding and fun, but it may not always be appropriate for you to carry out the work. Good assessment skills are required to determine which kind of help – family, individual or group work – will be the most effective intervention. After considering the needs of the bereaved child with whom you are working it may become clear that a combination of these would be beneficial so careful planning is essential. Knowledge of local resources may help you determine your course of action.

Key Points

- Family work is useful as the whole family is affected.
- Each family member will grieve at a different pace; family work may help members understand one another.
- Family sessions can be used to discuss practical issues.
- Individual work with children will allow them to work through their grief at their own level.
- Children often need space from the family to explore emotions and issues that might upset their parents or carers.
- Group work with children allows them to share with peers, fostering a sense of mutual identity and increasing self-esteem.

- It is helpful to explore the stages of grief, but not to expect children to resolve them all within the lifetime of the group.

- Careful consideration needs to be given to practical issues when planning a bereavement group.

CHAPTER 9

Guidelines for Effective Coping

The process of grieving can be long, hard and painful, whether you are the bereaved or whether you are someone working with the bereaved. There is much that can be done by others to help support you and much that one can do to support oneself. It is not a sign of weakness or failure to accept help, rather, it is a sign of courage and self-awareness that you acknowledge you have gone beyond your own resources and need help to carry on with the journey.

For the Bereaved

Learn to be gentle with yourself and give yourself plenty of time to grieve; don't rush. There are many things to be done, adjustments to be made and situations to come to terms with so don't expect yourself to be able to deal with too many things at once. Grief takes time, so do not fall into the trap of telling yourself you should be over it by now. Although it won't feel as acute as in the early stages, your mourning may take you through a period of years depending on your circumstances. Each new season, anniversary or special time without the deceased may revive feelings about the loss. As your children begin to find the strength to talk about what has happened, new pain may open up for you. Try to build a network of support to help you manage your grief and that of your children. It is sometimes difficult to cope with a grieving child when one can barely cope with oneself, so try *not* to cope on your own.

- Involve other people such as relatives, a teacher or a friend in giving support to your children.

- Sometimes children will find it easier to talk to someone outside of the family. Try not to see this as a failure. They may simply wish to express themselves to someone less emotionally involved.

- Take time to relax and enjoy yourself and not feel guilty about it. Try to go out and have fun with your children and friends.

- Do something to relax: a soak in the bath, a walk in the country, reading.

- Physical pursuits such as gardening, working out at the gym or running may help to release pent-up feelings.

By taking care of yourself you will have more energy to look after children who need more attention during bereavement. Having fun, laughing and enjoying yourself doesn't mean you don't care or that you have forgotten the deceased. Remember, you need 'time off' from grief sometimes just to be able to go on grieving.

For Bereavement Workers

It is important for anyone working with bereaved families to recognise the effects of such work on him- or herself. Being the receptor for many strong emotions can be damaging and stressful. The need to 'counsel the counsellors' has been highlighted by workers involved in counselling children and their families after disasters such as, the sinking of the *Herald of Free Enterprise*, or the Hillsborough football stadium tragedy. Workers involved in helping bereaved people need to offload feelings and receive support, as witnessing other people's suffering can leave you feeling helpless and overwhelmed at times.

Other people's grief can sometimes raise unresolved losses from your past and plunge you into emotional turmoil. Sometimes there is a risk of becoming over-involved, as the boundaries between the caregiver and the bereaved person become blurred. You can find yourself doing too much, giving too much time to one situation. Having empathy and being able to actively support and care for people and yet maintain a professional distance is remarkably hard at times. Support from colleagues, and supervision of your work by a manager is invaluable at these times. However, neither of these are of any use unless you can be honest with yourself about your needs. Knowing about yourself is essential in preventing inappropriate involvement with clients or 'burn-out', so take time to work on looking at yourself.

People working in community institutions, such as schools and residential homes, have particular problems to face. The support they are offering may involve large numbers of children all affected by one event, such as the death of a pupil or resident, or disasters involving the whole community. Not only are there the pupils or other residents to deal with, but there may also be the staff, parents or the whole community. You may well be dealing with the intrusion of the media too. One event can overwhelm the lives of many and you may suddenly find yourself dealing with many tasks.

It is at these times that particular care needs to be taken of workers. Staff whose needs are acknowledged and met will be remain happier in their work and be able to invest further energy in it. A lack of supportive structures may lead to staff experiencing 'burn-out' or suffering breakdowns. There may be an increase in the level of absenteeism from work through illness and there may be constant staff changes as disaffected workers leave. When people are working with children and families where there are bereavement issues they need:

- a strong management structure;
- opportunity for consultation;
- staff meetings;
- key workers;
- regular supervision;
- effective communication;
- clear policies;
- clear definition of roles and boundaries;
- recognition of personal boundaries as a caregiver/counsellor;
- recognition of the limitations of interventions.

Any adult working with bereaved children will need to acknowledge his or her own personal limitations. There is only so much one can do. There will be times when the task would be better accomplished if shared with another worker, or with a relative or friend of the bereaved child. Workers should be aware of resources in the community, such as Cruse Bereavement Care or Compassionate Friends, for whom the task may be more appropriate. It is also vital that one should be able to recognise when the time has come to refer the child on for more specialist help. It may be prudent to consider this if the child shows signs of:

- persistent anxieties about their own death;
- destructive outbursts;
- compulsive caregiving;
- euphoria;
- accident-proneness;

- a protracted period of unwillingness to speak about the deceased;
- expression of only positive or only negative feelings about the deceased person;
- inability or unwillingness to seek new relationships;
- daydreaming – resulting in poor academic performance;
- stealing;
- school phobia.

Conclusion

Working with bereaved children is challenging but rewarding. It is not all stress and strain; there can be times of laughter and fun as well as times of sadness and pain. To combat the latter in ourselves, we have to remember to be gentle with ourselves. Time spent away from the bereaved child is as important as time spent with them. Learning to relax, to switch off, in invest our energy in something else, helps with the management of stress and thus enables us to become more effective helpers when the situation demands it.

Key Points

- It is important for adults to recognise the effect on themselves of children's grief.
- It is important to build up a network of support.
- Try to involve others and so spread the task.
- It is important that caregivers give themselves time to relax and 'switch off'.
- Such work can make professionals feel helpless and powerless, so effective support systems are necessary.
- There can be a risk of boundaries becoming blurred.

- It is important for adults working with bereaved children to recognise their own limitations.
- Some children may need to be referred on for more specialist help.

References

Black, D. (1978) 'The bereaved child.' *Journal of Child Psychology and Psychiatry 19*, 287–292.

Black, D. (1993a) 'Traumatic bereavement in children.' *National Children's Bureau Highlight 121.*

Black, D. (1993b) *When Father Kills Mother.* London: Routledge.

Bowlby, J. (1969) *Attachment and Loss, Volume 1.* London: Hogarth Press.

Bowlby, J. (1973) *Attachment and Loss, Volume 2.* London: Hogarth Press.

Bowlby, J. (1979a) *The Making and Breaking of Affectional Bonds.* London: Tavistock

Bowlby, J. (1979b) 'On knowing what you are not supposed to know and feeling what you are not supposed to feel.' *Canadian Journal of Psychiatry 24*, 403–408.

Bowlby, J. (1980) *Attachment and Loss, Volume 3.* London: Hogarth Press.

Erikson, E. (1965) *Childhood and Society.* Harmondsworth: Penguin Books.

Furman, E. (1986) 'When is the death of a parent traumatic?' *Psychoanalytic Studies of the Child 41*, 191–208.

Kranzler, E.M., Shaffer, D., Wasseman, G. and Davies, M. (1990) 'Early childhood bereavement.' *Journal of the American Academy of Child and Adolescent Psychiatry 29*, 4, 513–520.

Pynoos, R. (1992) 'Grief and trauma in children and adolescents.' *Bereavement Care 11*, 1.

Pynoos, R. and Eth, S. (1984) 'The child as witness to homicide.' *The Journal for the Psychological Study of Social Issues 40*, 2, 87–108.

Pynoos, R. and Eth, S. (1986) 'Witness to violence: The child interview.' *Journal of the American Academy of Child Psychiatry 25*, 3, 306–319.

Pynoos, R. *et al.* (1987) 'Life threats and post traumatic stress in school age children.' *Archives of General Psychiatry 44*, 1057–1063.

Shears, J. (1995) 'Managing a tragedy in school.' In S. Smith and M. Pennells (eds) *Interventions with Bereaved Children.* London: Jessica Kingsley Publishers.

Siegal, D.J. (1997) 'Memory and trauma.' In D. Black (ed) *Psychological Trauma: A Developmental Approach.* London: Cassell.

Smith, S. and Pennells, M. (1993) 'Bereaved children and adolescents.' In K.N. Dwivedi (ed) *Group Work with Children and Adolescents.* London: Jessica Kingsley Publishers.

Terr, L. (1991) 'Childhood traumas: An outline and overview.' *American Journal of Psychiatry 148*, 1, 10–19.

Weller, E.B., Weller, R.A., Fristad, M., Cain, S. and Bowes, J. (1988) Should children attend their parent's funeral?' *Journal of the American Academy of Child and Adolescent Psychiatry 2*, 5, 559–562.

Resources

Book List
Books for younger children (4–12 years old)

Althea (1982) *When Uncle Bob Died.* London: Dinosaur Publications.

Bosal, S. (1997) *Something to Remember Me By.* Communication Project: Ontario, Canada.*

Burningham, J. (1990) *Grandpa.* London: Red Fox.

Connolly, M. (1999) *It Isn't Easy.* Oxford: Oxford University Press.

Curtis, C. (1993) *How Far to Heaven?* Washington USA: Illumination Arts.*

Gerstein, M. (1996) *Mountains of Tibet.* Bristol: Barefoot Books.*

Jones, J. (1987) *Dadi Maa Dies.* London: Blackie.

Joslin, M. (1998) *The Goodbye Boat.* Oxford: Lion Books.

Lanton, S. (1996) *Daddy's Chair.* Oxford: ABC Publications.

Levete, S. (1997) *When People Die.* London: Watts.

MacGregor, M. (1993) *The Sky Goes on Forever.* Washington, USA: Illumination Arts.*

Mellonie, B. and Ingpen, R. (1983) *Beginnings and Endings with Lifetimes in Between.* Limpsfield, Surrey: Dragons World Books.

Perkins, G. and Morris, L. (1996) *Remembering Mum.* London: A and C Black.

Rushton, L. (1992) *Death Customs.* East Sussex: Wayland.

Simmonds, P. (1987) *Fred.* London: Puffin.

Sims, A. (1986) *Am I Still a Sister?* Slidell, LA: Big A and Co.

Stickney, D. (1984) *Waterbugs and Dragonflies.* London: Mowbray.

Ure, J. (1997) *Becky Bananas: 'This is Your Life!'* London: Collins.

Varley, S. (1985) *Badger's Parting Gifts.* London: Collins (Lions).

White, E.B. (1963) *Charlotte's Web*. London: Puffin Books.

Wilhelm, H. (1985) *I'll Always Love You*. Kent: Hodder and Stoughton.

Books for teenagers

Abrams, R. (1993) *When Parents Die*. London: Letts.

Department of Social Work, St. Christopher's Hospice (1989) *Someone Special Had Died*. London: St. Christopher's Hospice. Available from St. Christopher's Hospice, 51–59 Lawrie Park Road, London SE22 6DZ.

Ehrlich, A. (1993) *The Dark Card*. London: Walker Books.

Guy, R. (1995) *The Friends*. London: Puffin Modern Classics.

Hospice of St. Francis (1990) *Young People and Bereavement*. Berkhamstead: St. Francis Hospice. (Available from Hospice of St. Francis, 27 Shrubland Road, Berkhamstead, Hertfordshire HP4 3HX.)

Kaye, G. (1995) *Comfort Herself*. London: Scholastic Press.

Krememtz, J. (1991) *How it Feels When a Parent Dies*. London: Gollancz.

Lloyd, C. (1989) *The Charlie Barber Treatment*. London: Walker Books.

Nystrom, C. (1990) *Emma Says Goodbye*. Oxford: Lion Books.

Roy, J. (1996) *A Daughter Like Me*. London: Puffin Books.

Walker, A. (1988) *To Hell with Dying*. Kent: Hodder and Stoughton.

Wallbank, S. (1991) *Facing Grief: Bereavement and the Young Adult*. Cambridge: Lutterworth Press.

Williams, G. and Ross, J. (1983) *When People Die*. Edinburgh: Macdonald.

Books for professionals

Duffy, Wendy (1991) *The Bereaved Child: A Guide for Teachers and Leaders*. The National Society of the Church of England.

Dyregov, A. (1991) *Grief in Children*. London: Jessica Kingsley Publishers.

Geldard, K. and Geldard, D. (1997) *Counselling Children: A Practical Introduction*. London: Sage.

Grollman, E. (ed.) (1969) *Explaining Death to Children*. Boston, MA: Beacon Press.

Heegaard, M. (1988) *When Someone Very Special Dies*. Minneapolis, MN: Woodland Press.

Jewett, C. (1994) *Helping Children Cope with Separation and Loss*. Boston, MA: Harvard Common Press.

Perschy, M.K. (1997) *Helping Teens Work through Grief.* London: Taylor and Francis Ltd.

Rando, T. (1984) *Grief, Death and Dying.* Champaign, IL: Research Press Co.

Smith, S. and Pennells, M. (1995) *Interventions with Bereaved Children.* London: Jessica Kingsley Publishers.

Staudacher, C. (1988) *Beyond Grief.* London: Souvenir Press.

Turner, M. (1998) *Talking with Children and Young People about Death and Dying.* London: Jessica Kingsley Publishers.

Understanding Death and Dying: Booklets for People with Learning Disabilities, their Families and Carers. Kidderminster: British Institute of Learning Disabilities.

Ward, B. *et al.* (1995) *Good Grief 1: Exploring Feelings, Loss and Death with Under Elevens, 2nd Edition.* London: Jessica Kingsley Publishers.

Ward, B. *et al.* (1996) *Good Grief 2: Exploring Feelings, Loss and Death with Over Elevens and Adults, 2nd Edition.* London: Jessica Kingsley Publishers.

Wells, R. (1988) *Helping Children Cope with Grief.* London: Sheldon Press.

Worden, J.W. (1983) *Grief Counselling and Grief Therapy, 2nd Edition.* London: Routledge.

Worden, J.W. (1996) *Children and Grief: When a Parent Dies.* New York: Guildford Press.

* Available from Words of Discovery, 15 The Tythings, Kibworth Beauchamp, Leicester LE8 0PU.

Videos

1. *That Morning I went to School*
2. *Childhood Grief*

Both videos can be bought or hired from:
The Child, Adolescent and Family Service
8 Notre Dame Mews
Northampton NN1 2BG
Phone: 01604 604608

Someone Died, It Happened to Me
Available from:
The Child Bereavement Trust
Harleyford Estate
Henley Road
Marlow
Buckinghamshire SL7 2DX
Phone: 01628 488101

Where's Pete?
The Fall of Feddy the Leaf
The Tenth Good Thing About Barney
All available from:
Educational Media International
235 Imperial Drive
Harrow
Middlesex HA2 7HE
Phone 0181 868 1908

Giving Sorrow Words – Managing Bereavement in Schools
(Video and Resource Manual) Available from:
Video Inset
PO Box 197
Cardiff CF5 2WF
Phone 01222 405689
Email: video.inset"@net.ntl.com.

Useful Addresses

Cruse Bereavement Care
126 Sheen Road
Richmond
Surrey TW9 1UR

The Child Bereavement Trust
Harleyford Estate
Henley Road
Marlow
Buckinghamshire SL7 2DX

The Compassionate Friends
6 Denmark Street
Bristol, BS1 5DQ

The National Association of Bereavement Services
20 Norton Folgate
London E1 6DB

Index